Secret Gadgets and Strange Gizmos

HIGH-TECH (AND LOW-TECH) INNOVATIONS OF THE U.S. MILITARY

BILL YENNE

ZENITH PRESS

First published in 2005 by Zenith Press, an imprint of
MBI Publishing Company, Galtier Plaza, Suite 200,
380 Jackson Street, St. Paul, MN 55101-3885 USA

Zenith Press titles are also available at discounts in bulk quantity for
industrial or sales-promotional use. For details write to Special Sales
Manager at MBI Publishing Company, Galtier Plaza, Suite 200,
380 Jackson Street, St. Paul, MN 55101-3885 USA.

ISBN-13: 978-0-7603-2115-7
ISBN-10: 0-7603-2115-9

Editors: Steve Gansen and Lindsay Hitch
Designer: Tom Heffron

Printed in China

On the frontispiece:
A model poses with a Hughes GAR-2 (AIM-4) missile, the precursor to
the AIM-26 Nuclear Falcon, at Edwards Air Force Base on December 17,
1956. In the background, Test Pilot Robert G. Laurence waits in the cockpit
of a Convair F-102 Delta Dagger. Both the AIM-4 and AIM-26 were
operational aboard the F-102. *Author's collection*

On the title page:
The Convair Lobber was a solid-fuel, surface-to-surface missile designed
to carry supplies. It was designed so that the missile and its launcher could
be carried by a three-man team. It was about nine feet long and had a ten-
inch diameter. The Lobber could hurl fifty pounds of supplies about eight
miles. These field tests were carried out by the U.S. Army in December
1958. *Author's collection*

On the table of contents:
One of the unsung heroines among the gadgets and gear of the Cold War,
Stratoflex tubing was widely used by the aerospace industry. When this
advertising appeared in the early 1960s, it was confidently predicted that
Stratoflex would be present when humans reached the moon. It is a good
idea that NASA chose not to use this space suit design for the Apollo
program. *Author's collection*

On the back cover, clockwise from top left:
Poised for takeoff, this man is ready for a tethered test of the Redstone
small rocket lift device. *Redstone Arsenal*

With a parabolic concentrator on her head, this young civil defense spotter
is ready to locate the sounds of approaching aircraft. She'll use her
binoculars to identify them. If they are from an enemy nation, the
authorities will soon know. *Author's collection*

First fielded in 1917, this unique American one-man tank was intended to
be used by scouts. So as to appear innocuous on the littered battlefield of
no-man's land, it was designed to look like a damaged artillery piece.
It was equipped with a wire cutter for getting through the masses of
barbed wire strewn across the Western front, but it did not offer protection
for the operator's legs! *Author's collection*

About the author:
   Bill Yenne is the San Francisco–based author of more than two dozen
books on military, aviation, and historical topics. He is a member of the
American Aviation Historical Society and the American Society of
Journalists and Authors, as well as a graduate of the Stanford University
Professional Publishing Course. A regular contributor to the *World Airpower
Review*, Yenne is the author of *The Story of the Boeing Company*, as well as
histories of several other important planemakers, including Convair and
Lockheed.
   His other works include *Attack of the Drones: A History of Unmanned
Aerial Combat; Secret Weapons of the Cold War; Secret Weapons of World
War II; The History of the U.S. Air Force;* and *SAC: A Primer of Strategic Air
Power.* Of *SAC*, Major Michael Perini wrote in *Air Force Magazine*, "This
book deserves a place on any airman's bookshelf and in the stacks of
serious military libraries."
   Yenne was also a contributor and aviation consultant to *The Simon
and Schuster D-Day Encyclopedia*. He worked with the legendary U.S. Air
Force commander General Curtis E. LeMay to produce *Superfortress: The
B-29 and American Airpower in World War II*, which *Publishers Weekly*
described as "An eloquent tribute."

CONTENTS

ACKNOWLEDGMENTS

I wish to thank all of the people, agencies, and institutions who provided material used in this book. Special thanks are due to Michael Monnett of the Oak Ridge National Laboratory, Noel McCormack of the NRO Center for the Study of National Reconnaissance, and Eric Shulzinger of Lockheed Martin, who provided me with a large number of images from that firm and from the Lockheed and Martin heritage companies.

Shown here is a Martin Marietta Electronics electro-optical tracking and guidance module for the Low-Level Air Defense System (LLADS), circa 1991. *Martin Marietta*

INTRODUCTION

Often in the history of technological innovation, military necessity has been the mother of invention. Times of war have also served as catalysts for an unusually large number of important inventions. In the twentieth century, periods of warfare, both cold and hot, saw rapid advances on a number of technological fronts. Many of these would probably not have happened in so fast or well-funded a manner had it not been for the backdrop of international tension and open hostilities. Examples from World War II, for example, range from jet propulsion to radar, from the ubiquitous use of antibiotics to what was once fondly called "the power of the atom."

Numerous books have chronicled the great weapons of the wars since the start of the twentieth century—World War I, World War II, the Cold War, and the Gulf Wars. And countless books have been written on individual aircraft, tanks, warships, and infantry weapons. This book looks the other way, toward the unusual, secret, unheralded, and forgotten—the inventions that are often unrecalled in their military context. This is a survey of some of the lesser-known weapons and military systems that have come about in the century since the United States entered World War I. This is not a systematic study, but rather a random collection that unfolds like a visit to the attic—or the roadside museum—of military history.

You will find the wonderful stacked next to the dreadful, the preposterous adjacent to the deadly serious. Some items in this attic were mass-produced, while others were one of a kind. Things you may be familiar with will be cheek by jowl with things you may never have imagined.

As you make your way through the narrow, crowded corridors, you'll see small handheld gear on shelves next to those groaning under the weight of enormous weapons. The final chapter covers weapons that became household words later in the twenty-first century or were long forgotten by mid-century.

You might find yourself asking, "What were they thinking?" one moment, and "Why didn't they think of this before?" the next. We hope that whatever you think, your tour will be an interesting one.

The three technicians shown here in protective clothing have just emerged from cleaning in the residual toxic mercury atmosphere within the seventy-foot structure seen in the center. The toxic mercury remained after ion-engine testing. The photograph was taken in the 1960s at the Lewis Research Center's Electric Propulsion Laboratory (since renamed as the John H. Glenn Research Center) in Cleveland, Ohio. *NASA*

CHAPTER ONE

WORLD WAR I

The great powers that fell headlong into World War I did so with their high commands operating under the naïve illusion that military technology had advanced little since the nineteenth century. They foresaw flags and cavalry charges, and an armistice perhaps as early as Christmas 1914. As many books have chronicled, reality could not have been further from this fantasy. What lay ahead was four years of the most hellish carnage the world had ever seen. Millions bled their life away in the stalemate trench warfare of the eastern front on a scale that nobody could have predicted.

The first World War was called many things. Because it was the largest conflict yet experienced, or certainly the largest to have consumed Europe, it was called the Great War. Because of its global scope, it was called the World War. For a hopeful and naïve American president, Woodrow Wilson, it was the war to end all wars. And for students of military weaponry, World War I was the first modern war.

A host of weapons systems that are integral to modern military engagement either made their battlefield debut or saw first wide-scale use

during World War I. Submarines and aircraft had seen limited use in combat before 1914, but they both changed the nature of warfare in World War I. By this standard, one might also call World War I the first "three-dimensional war."

The nature of combat in the World War I was also defined by the use of tanks and machine guns. The conflict also saw the widespread use of poison gas, a weapon that made so terrible an impression on the combatants that it was not used in combat during World War II, except by the Japanese against the Chinese.

Most of the major weapons systems of World War I are well documented, but the war also gave us many lesser known and often amusing weapons, such as those included in this chapter. As during the century's later wars, there were strange, often ludicrous proposals for weapons that embodied technology that had yet to be created. There was a proposal to freeze clouds and use airplanes to position artillery atop them so Allied guns would have the high ground. Other very strange artillery proposals included an enormous concrete pump to hurl a stream of concrete across no-man's land to fill

Above: Among the unusual gear studied for the protection of American troops in World War I was this strangely camouflaged uniform being modeled by a man from Company F of the 24th Engineers. It might have worked better if he had been among tree branches. *U.S. Army*

Opposite page: This helmet modification using a chain fringe was designed to protect the eyes of the wearer from splinters of metal, wood, or stone. While the British-style helmet was adopted as standard by the U.S. Army, the E. J. Codd Company of Baltimore modified a French helmet for this prototype. Note the *RF* for *République Française*. *U.S. Army/War Department*

Arguably more practical than a chain fringe for eye protection is this screen visor. It could be raised or lowered, and cupped beneath the nose to protect against ricocheting fragments. *Author's collection*

Developed by Clarence Stocks, this complex helmet involved two layers, with shutters for the eye holes and a spring between the layers to reduce the shock from shrapnel hitting the outer layer. It certainly covered the head and eyes, but it was criticized for offering a narrow field of view and for being hot and cumbersome. *Author's collection*

These three soldiers were participants in a U.S. Army Ordnance Department evaluation of medieval-style body armor conducted at Langres, France, in 1918. Note the effect of pistol, rifle, and machine gun fire, and imagine the weight of the armor. *U.S. Army*

the German trenches. There was also a suggestion to use artillery shells to drop containers of snakes into German trenches.

A proposal that was actually advanced during World War I suggested suspending giant magnets from balloons to pluck German rifles and machine guns out of enemy trenches. Preposterous as it seems in hindsight, it was also seriously suggested that vultures be trained to pick the mortar out of brick smokestacks, and that such birds be sent to German industrial cities to topple smokestacks. One of the most bizarre gadgets that was suggested—although there is no known science to support such a weapon—involved a means to blot out the moon to prevent German bombers from being able to fly missions at night. The idea was simple: If searchlights using white light could be used for illumination, why couldn't a black light be beamed at the moon to put it in darkness? This is a question that has yet to be answered.

But science has a way of catching up with ideas that seemed ridiculous at the time. During World War I, a number of scientists proposed the use of electromagnetic guns. At the end of the century, electromagnetic guns, now called railguns, were the subject of intense study by the United States Strategic Defense Initiative Office, and we'll discuss them in a later chapter. The electromagnetic guns proposed during World War I had a basis

in scientific fact, and such a gun had already been patented by the great Norwegian-born explorer and inventor Kristian Birkeland. Before the war, Birkeland had designed and test-fired an electromagnetic gun, achieving a muzzle velocity of 325 feet per second and a range of about a kilometer. None of his guns were actually used in the war, however.

Among the many new weapons that were used for the first time, we highlight some that were deployed on a limited basis and others that were proposals and prototypes, and we revisit a selection of the overshadowed and forgotten footnotes of World War I.

Helmets and Body Armor

Body armor has been used in conflicts from antiquity through the Middle Ages until today. In the eighteenth and nineteenth centuries, however, it fell into disuse. The extra weight entailed was eschewed in favor of lightness and mobility. In World War I, because of the advent of the ubiquitous machine gun and the constant danger of shrapnel from exploding shells, armor once again seemed like a good idea.

Helmets became standard equipment during World War I, and they have remained so ever since. Britain, France, and Germany each adopted a unique design based on their interpretation of what would work best. While the German design was seen as perhaps the best in terms of protection, the United States adopted the British design because it was lighter and easier to mass produce. It weighed just two pounds.

The helmet was not intended to stop a direct hit from a rifle or machine-gun round, but to protect the wearer from shrapnel, which was much more likely to do harm than a rare well-placed bullet. A helmet

This young doughboy is fitted out in an experimental suit of armor that included a standard helmet with a visor, plus a sixteen-pound suit of armor which covers about as much of his body as does modern standard-issue Kevlar. *Author's collection*

The suit of armor designed in 1917 by Otis Boucher would have given the doughboy a strange appearance, like something from a 1950s science fiction film. The padded steel helmet offered a limited field of view, but significant protection from shrapnel. *Author's collection*

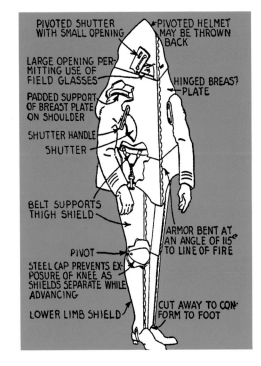

This cutaway illustration of the Otis Boucher body armor shows how the pieces bolted together. The legs were armored, but not the arms. *Author's collection*

with metal four times as thick as the standard helmet would have been required to stop a direct bullet hit. A helmet this thick and heavy was deemed impractical for use in battle.

Because the eyes were unprotected by the helmet, various modifications were considered to shelter the eyes from splinters of metal, wood, and stone. One system developed by the E. J. Codd Company of Baltimore involved a fringe consisting of short lengths of fairly heavy chain

attached to the rim of the helmet. Such an arrangement was an adaptation of the chain doors then used in factories where metal and glass fragments were a hazard. To this day, chain and chain mail fireplace screens are common.

The search for body armor led to a variety of experiments, including some that revisited the

When not being worn, the versatile Otis Boucher body armor could be erected vertically and used as a firing shield. *Author's collection*

armor used by the knights of the fifteenth and sixteenth centuries. Such designs were effective against shrapnel, but not against machine-gun rounds. Though many body-armor schemes were advanced, none were deemed sufficiently practical to be adopted for widespread use. This was mainly due to weight, because armor that could stop bullets would have weighed fifty-five pounds. Indeed, it was not until the advent of Kevlar body armor in the latter part of the twentieth century that any such type of gear became standard.

Unusual Tanks and Armored Vehicles

Tanks and armored vehicles made their operational debut in World War I. Numerous configurations of tanks were designed and fielded as tacticians and weapons designers grappled with the question of exactly what a tank should look like. It was a given that they should be heavily armed and armored, and that they should run on caterpillar tractor treads. Aside from that, many configurations were studied and tested, often in live combat.

Unusual Artillery Shells

Of the millions of artillery shells fired during World War I, most carried a high-explosive charge. Others carried alternate deadly agents, including poison gas. The payloads of still other shells are amazingly similar in concept to some of the kinetic-energy weapons that were considered by the Strategic Defense Initiative Office in the 1980s and the National Missile Defense Agency in the twenty-first century. One such shell was packed

These U.S. Marine Corps recruits are wearing mesh helmets and padded body armor that were designed not for actual combat, but for bayonet training. *Kadel & Herbert*

with heavy chains designed to rip through barbed-wire entanglements as if they were spiderwebs. Yet another was designed to deploy masses of barbed wire when fired into a group of attacking enemy troops or into a trench. Such a shell would create hellish pain and havoc when it exploded.

Probably the strangest artillery shell ever designed was the Andrew Graham shell, which

Looking like a prop from a science fiction film, the bowl-shaped land monitor was one of history's strangest tanks, though inside it was fairly conventional. The mushroom-shaped design was said to remind soldiers of the fixed gun emplacements that the Germans had erected around Liège, Belgium. The monitor weighed 7.5 tons, had a top speed of six miles per hour, and stood eight feet tall. An innovative feature was that its entire hull, twelve feet in diameter, rotated like a modern tank turret. It is seen here as being roomy for three, but it had a crew complement of eight. *Author's collection*

This 1917 tricycle tank was one of several such configurations studied in the United States during World War I. The idea was that the forward wheel would serve to steer the big machine. In practice, the wheel was more prone to becoming stuck in the mud than treads. This particular tank had a high center of gravity and was prone to tipping over when climbing a steep embankment. *International Film Service*

contained twelve loaded rifle barrels. The shell would be fired at enemy aircraft, and when in their vicinity, fire a barrage of .30-caliber projectiles. The concept was extremely innovative, but issues with aiming and timing proved insurmountable.

Parachutes

Aerial combat was one of the most memorable and colorful types of engagement in World War I. Aviation technology advanced rapidly in many respects. Excellent aircraft and powerful engines evolved, as did the means to arm aircraft. For example, synchronization devices allowed fighter pilots to fire through the arc of a turning propeller.

One major feature of aerial combat separated World War I from World War II and later wars: airplane pilots didn't carry parachutes. The crews of dirigibles and observation balloons were equipped with parachutes, but it was easy to step out of a balloon basket, and it was another thing entirely to successfully exit a fast-moving airplane with a bulky parachute. During World War I, the combatants designed and

First fielded in 1917, this unique American one-man tank was intended to be used by scouts. So as to appear innocuous on the littered battlefield of no-man's land, it was designed to look like a damaged artillery piece. It was equipped with a wire cutter for getting through the masses of barbed wire strewn across the Western front, but it did not offer protection for the operator's legs! *Author's collection*

The Felicetti one-man tank was propelled by means of a spade-like pusher mechanism on the sides and steered by the operator's feet. It was essentially a cross between a tank and body armor. Claustrophobia sufferers should not have volunteered for this duty. *Author's collection*

One of the most interesting American military vehicles of World War I was this gyroscopically controlled, powered unicycle. Levers controlled the steering by shifting the gyroscope, which was vacuum sealed in its case and powered by a storage battery. The operator sat ahead of the wheel to balance the weight of the one-cylinder engine. *Author's collection*

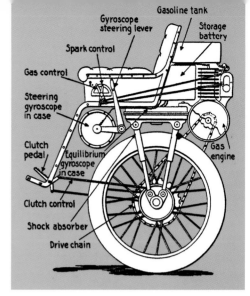

explored various methods of escaping an airplane with a parachute.

Life Preservers

Many of the gadgets developed for the United States armed services during World War I were as much about saving lives as taking them. As with parachutes for use aboard airplanes, life preservers for use aboard ships were of continuing interest to the U.S. Navy. Various innovative designs ranged from mattresses filled with kapok to self-inflating gas bags.

Beam-Sight Pistol

Today, the use of a laser rifle sight for pinpointing targets at great distance is routine for both military snipers and assassins. The idea is not new, having originated with an ingenious system developed during World War I. This precursor to the modern system used an inventive system to switch on the light. The wiring that connected the battery to the lightbulb passed through a chamber containing a small amount of mercury, which, being a metal, is an electrical conductor. When the revolver was brought level for firing, the mercury would flow in such a way as to complete the circuit, illuminating the light. Presumably, the user of the gun would know not to rely on the light for aiming at targets above or below him. The light would have had a wider beam than a laser, making it easier for the user to be seen in the dark when it was on.

Mobile Signal Towers

Today we take wireless communications for granted, but in World War I that term had an entirely different meaning. During that conflict, as in previous conflicts dating back to the Middle Ages and before, communicators often had to rely on line of sight. Telegraph communications had been used in the Civil War, and field telephones were available in World War I, but both systems depended on wires that had to be installed and could be cut or easily tapped.

As low-tech as it was, semaphore signaling was more versatile. The operator depended on

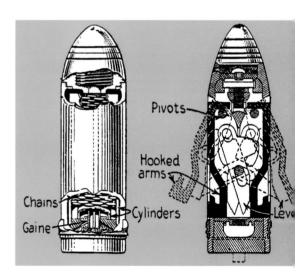

Two artillery shells designed for the common purpose of tearing up barbed wire entanglements operated on different principles. The one on the left contained heavy chains that were spun out to create a scythe-like action. The one on the right had hooked cutting arms that were deployed by an explosive charge to create a scissors-like tool that would slice through barbed wire. *Author's collection*

Looking like the rocket pods used on modern attack aircraft and helicopters, this shell was designed by Andrew Graham in 1917 to fire rifle bullets at enemy aircraft. Considering that the trajectory of the bullets would have been parallel to that of the shell, aiming would have been highly problematic. *Author's collection*

Barbed wire could be deployed instantly or used as an offensive weapon through the use of this mortar shell designed in Detroit by Enid Wales. The shell contained five canisters of tightly spooled barbed wire, which was released through individual explosive charges detonated by a time fuse. The canisters would deploy their wire in separate directions. *International Film Service*

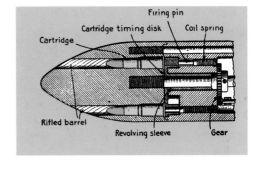

high ground so the signal could be seen at long distances. Mobile signal towers offered an army the flexibility of having portable high ground. The tower could be extended up to about twenty-five feet and driven anywhere that it was need-ed, and it could be folded down for going under low bridges. It could also be adapted for use as a radio-transmission tower. The downside was that the semaphore man was vulnerable to snipers while on his perch.

Floating Fortresses

During World War I, a number of proposals were advanced for developing floating fortresses for defending ports and other waterways. The con-cept evolved from the notion of arming light buoys with heavy machine guns and artillery. An opera-tor or operators could be stationed aboard such buoys and could engage approaching enemy warships. Given that such a fortress would be extremely vulnerable to enemy fire because its operators could not take evasive action, measures were taken to permit the buoys to submerge.

Valves and compressed-air tanks would have taken time to operate in an emergency submersion,

so the concept gradually evolved into offshore fortresses that could be permanently submerged except during resupply and crew changes. The offensive weapons were to have been torpedoes, which would have been more effective against enemy warships than guns. Submerged fortresses could also have been made larger than ones that floated on the surface. Such weapons are not believed to have been deployed.

Intelligent Rifles

In the last decades of the twentieth century, the term smart bomb entered the lexicon of modern warfare, and the concept of artificial intelligence has been floating around the data-processing world for decades. The idea is that non-human mechanisms can calculate the means of achiev-ing an objective. An early definition of artificial intelligence was offered by John McCarthy at the 1956 Dartmouth Artificial Intelligence Con-ference, when he described it as "making a machine behave in ways that would be called intelligent if a human were so behaving."

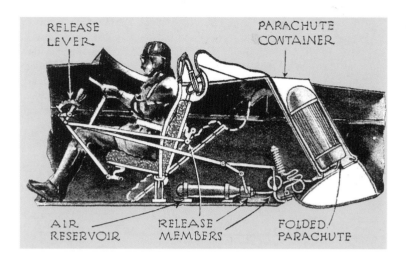

RELEASE LEVER

PARACHUTE CONTAINER

AIR RESERVOIR

RELEASE MEMBERS

FOLDED PARACHUTE

The Calthrop parachute system was a precursor of the modern ejection seat. A compressed air bottle fired the parachute container into the slipstream, where it would instantly inflate, pulling the pilot out of the aircraft. *Author's collection*

We tend to think of artificial intelligence and smart weapons as late-twentieth-century phenomena. However, in World War I, three aiming systems for infantry rifles pioneered this idea. The German Müller rifle and the American Eley rifle used an adjustable pendulum system to pull the trigger when the gun was aimed properly and to lock the trigger when the gun was at an incorrect elevation. Captain Eley, who developed the gun, is not to be confused with Eley, Ltd., of Cordfield, England, which today is a major manufacturer of .22-caliber sporting ammunition.

The French Bourdells rifle placed an electromagnet in the stock to fire the gun. The flow of current to the magnet was controlled by an ampoule of mercury, which allowed the current to pass only when the rifle was at the proper angle. As the phrase goes, "You can't miss."

Offensive Water Jackets

In World War I, the British army issued flotation devices to soldiers who couldn't swim so that

The McLaughlin parachute was one of several that were designed to be worn atop the head of the pilot. It would be deployed by opening it into the slipstream. It would then jerk the pilot out of the airplane—probably breaking his neck! *Author's collection*

they wouldn't drown when crossing streams or canals. When the U.S. Army deployed to France in 1917, Yankee ingenuity turned these life preservers into offensive weapons. The idea was that soldiers could be positioned in waterways and attack the enemy from these positions. The Germans would not have expected fire from a nearby canal. The downside for the floating infantry was that they would be easy prey for enemy gunners when they began shooting. Unlike the trenches, the water in the canals offered little protection from machine-gun fire. The phrase sitting duck easily comes to mind.

Lighted Torpedoes

The problem with launching a torpedo attack at night against enemy ships running under black-out conditions is obvious. In the days before radar and night-vision devices, target ships turned out their lights on all but the most moonlit of nights, and they were virtually invisible. To address this situation, Alphonse Fernandez developed a torpedo in which an arc light replaced the explosive charge. A timer would switch on the light after the torpedo was a safe distance from the launching vessel. Such torpedoes were to have been gyroscopically maneuvered until they located their

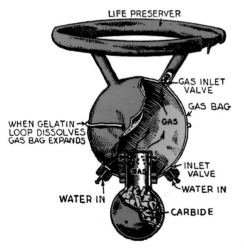

LIFE PRESERVER

GAS INLET VALVE

GAS BAG

GAS

WHEN GELATIN LOOP DISSOLVES GAS BAG EXPANDS

INLET VALVE

WATER IN

WATER IN

CARBIDE

This ingenious life preserver was based on the principal of using water as the catalyst for the chemical reaction that would cause it to inflate. As designed in Chicago by Kurt Nebel, the unit is worn with the tube around the waist, tied together by a water-soluble gelatin cord. When the wearer goes overboard, the valve sends water into contact with calcium carbide, filling the bag with acetylene gas. Unfortunately, acetylene is both toxic and extremely flammable. *Author's collection*

These recruits at the U.S. Navy's Newport Naval Training Station in Rhode Island are seen in April 1917 wearing kapok-filled mattresses designed to double as life preservers in the event that they had to abandon ship.
War Department

target. At that point, armed torpedoes could be launched.

Brévaire Acetylene Mortar

One of the first infantry weapons to use explosive gas rather than explosive solids—such as gunpowder—was the muzzle-loading acetylene mortar. It was designed in 1917 by R. A. Brévaire for use by troops in the trenches. After pressurized air and acetylene were let into the combustion chamber, ignition was by means of a simple spark plug. The shells were spin-stabilized by means of fins or vanes. The highly explosive nature of pressurized acetylene made it a dangerous substance to have stockpiled in an environment where shells and rifle bullets were flying.

At first glance, it looks like a radio tower, but the mobile signal tower of World War I was considerably less technologically advanced. It was actually a system of placing a semaphore signalman twenty-five feet above the ground any place that a car could be driven.
Author's collection

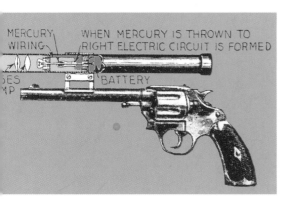

Somewhat more cumbersome than its modern laser analog, the flashlight pistol of 1917 used a self-lighting flashlight and an ingenuous mercury switch. *Author's collection*

This is one of the many proposals for floating fortresses conceived during World War I to protect channels and harbors. In this case, the fort was a turret that rotated on a permanently anchored base. Seasickness would have been a nagging problem as the fortresses bobbed in the tidal currents of a harbor entrance.
Author's collection

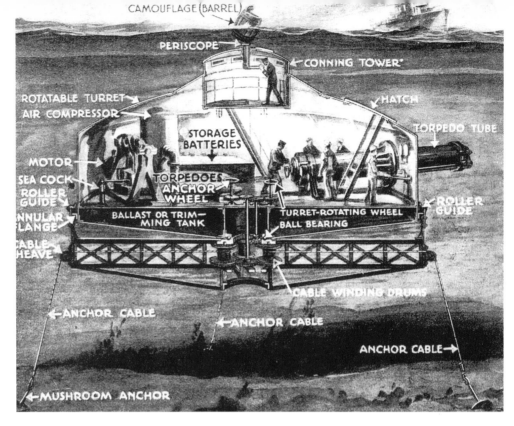

The American Eley rifle utilized a pendulum-activated trigger-locking device to fire the gun when it was aimed properly. The French Bourdells system used a mercury-controlled electromagnet to fire the weapon when it was elevated at a preset elevation. In both cases, the rifleman could adjust for range and angle of fire.
Author's collection

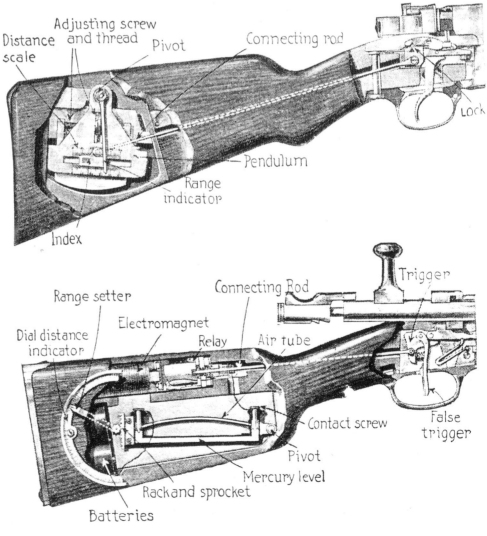

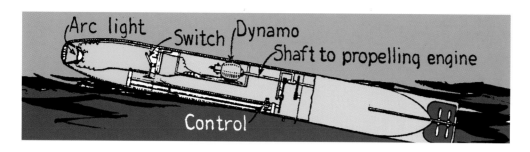

The Fernandez arc-light torpedo operated with its prow out of the water so that the beam of light was just a few degrees above the surface. *Author's collection*

Combination Trench Mirror and Cigarette Case

Not a weapon, but certainly a valuable piece of equipment for the doughboys in the trenches, was George Darling's remarkable magnifying trench mirror that doubled as a cigarette case. These mirrors were silver plated and carried a five-year warranty. For a dollar, Darling's manufacturing company in Providence, Rhode Island, would send them to a purchaser in the United States, or post them directly to the soldiers overseas or in stateside training camps. One wonders how many were around five years after Johnny came marching home, and how many are still sitting in drawers today.

Paravanes

Held in utmost secrecy during World War I was the paravane, a torpedo-like device used in mine sweeping. Fitted with fins and vanes and towed

This was not a lifesaving device, but a means of turning an infantryman into a warship! *International Film Service*

The Brévaire acetylene mortar was a tricky weapon to operate. The acetylene was highly explosive, and so noisy that a silencing mechanism was required. *Author's collection*

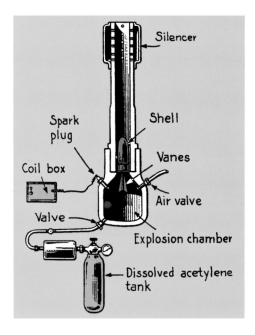

by a ship, the paravane is used to both deflect mines and to cut their mooring lines. The term was coined in the early twentieth century from a combination of parasol and vane. Paravanes were deployed from both sides of the bow of a ship passing through suspected minefields. Wings kept the paravane away from the sides of the ship. A depth-control valve, based on that of a torpedo, controlled rudder-like devices on the aft end to determine how deep the paravane would travel. When the cable anchoring the paravane to the ship caught the mooring cable of the mine, it pulled the mine toward the paravane, where the cable would be cut.

During World War I, paravanes were referred to by the British as PVs, and by the Yanks as otters. They continue to be used in mine sweeping and have been adapted as roll-damping systems in

The combination trench mirror and cigarette case was widely marketed to soldiers and their families. *Author's collection*

A crew of gobs aboard a U.S. Navy warship prepares to deploy a paravane, circa 1918. Paravanes remained top secret until after the Armistice. *International Film Service*

The mobile carrier pigeon loft was developed for deployment to the Western front as a base of operations. It housed seventy-five pigeons in wire cages. The pigeons were boxed and sent into the field strapped to dogs, as shown. *Author's collection*

civilian vessels, especially fishing trawlers. Para-vane stabilizers are used to reduce the rolling motion of a ship to improve comfort and reduce crew fatigue, although they do not improve the stability of the vessel.

Carrier Pigeons

The use of carrier pigeons to transmit messages in wartime is an innovative form of technology that dates back to the twelfth century, when the birds are recorded to have been used in, of all places, Baghdad. It is also known that they were used by Genghis Khan in the thirteenth century. Carrier pigeons, also known as messenger pigeons, are similar to homing pigeons, and all are domesticated breeds of Columbia livia, the bird that most people simply call pigeons, but which ornithologists call rock doves. What these breeds have in common is that they can find their way home from extremely long distances. Indeed, flights of more than a thousand miles and speeds in excess of thirty miles per hour have been recorded. When people discovered this, they utilized the birds to carry small pieces of paper with messages. The bird was simply taken away from home and released. It would then fly home with the message.

In the civilian world, Paul Reuter, the man who founded the Reuters news agency, used a fleet of four dozen carrier pigeons to deliver news and stock prices in Belgium in the 1850s. One bird named Cher Ami, which was used by the French forces in the war, was awarded the Croix de Guerre for heroically delivering important messages, including one that was delivered after Cher Ami had been nicked by a bullet.

While the extensive use of carrier pigeons ended with World War I, India actually maintained a police pigeon service messenger system in the state of Orissa until 2002!

U.S. Army Signal Corps personnel attach a message to a carrier pigeon near the front lines, circa 1918. *U.S. Army*

CHAPTER TWO
WORLD WAR II

★ ★ ★ ★ ★

**SOME ARMY OR NAVY
★ MAN'S USING IT NOW!**

● Some Army or Navy
★ man's probably using the
Powerlite you would like
to buy today—thousands
are in use in the Armed
★ Forces. Delta's two plants
are producing entirely for
war. But, when the war is
won there'll be Powerlites
★ again—better if there's a
way to make 'em better.
DELTA ELECTRIC CO.
★ **Marion, Indiana**

★ *Delta* POWER*lite* ★

★ ★ ★ ★ ★ ★ ★ ★ ★ ★

The second World War saw a burst of technological progress unprecedented in the history of warfare. From nuclear weapons to jet propulsion, World War II marked the most important turning point in military technology in the history of warfare. For example, many air forces were still flying open-cockpit biplanes when the war began, but by the time the war ended, jets were in service in the German, British, and U.S. air forces. The weapons that would define the Cold War—nuclear devices and long-range ballistic missiles—were born in World War II. Colossus, generally recognized as the world's first electronic computer, was created to break Germany's Enigma code.

The war started with aircraft carriers being a novelty and ended with carrier warfare having defined the future of naval power for the rest of the century. Radar was a major technological breakthrough that was virtually unknown when the war began. By 1940, land-based radar was playing a pivotal role in winning the Battle of Britain. By 1944, radar was equipping night-flying aircraft and allowing them to fight in complete darkness. The night-fighting aircraft of

1945 have more in common with the all-weather aircraft of today than they do with the warplanes of 1939.

There were bizarre secret projects such as spaceplanes and sound cannons. As strange as they seem, both of these weapons were actually being built in Germany when the Allies smashed their way across the borders of the Third Reich. Many of the strangest weapons were merely forgotten, while others remained secret for decades. The Ultra program that developed Colossus, and indeed the existence of this computer itself, was not revealed until 1974. The work of the Navajo code talkers—one of the most low-tech secret projects of the war—was not declassified until 1968, a quarter-century after they went into action. Germany's supersubmarines were developed under a tight cloak of secrecy that kept the details from being known until the war was long over.

We've chosen a wide range of strange and forgotten weapons from the attic of 1940s. Included here are some of America's earliest guided missiles. Germany is generally credited with having taken the technological lead in this

Above: Familiar to people in rural areas from the early part of the twentieth century through the 1960s, the ubiquitous Delta Electric Power Lite lanterns went overseas with the troops during World War II. The Delta Electric Company also produced bicycle lights and horn buttons, as well as postwar Christmas-tree lights. *Author's collection*

Opposite page: A technician checks the unique tail surfaces of the Douglas VB-10 Roc II. The program that had begun in 1940 as the supersecret Project MX-601 culminated in the 1943 rollout of the Roc II. This television-guided weapon would later be complemented by the infrared-guided VB-11 Roc III and the visually guided VB-13 Roc IV. *Douglas Aircraft*

field, but American designers were amazingly close behind with some great ideas of their own.

Roc

Named for the enormous bird of Arabian mythology, the radar-guided Roc I was acquired by the U.S. Army Air Forces under the vertical bomb designation VB-9. The Douglas Aircraft Company began building guided missiles during World War II (as was the case with McDonnell, with whom Douglas would merge in 1967). Such work had begun as early as 1940 under the secret Project MX-601. This program included the development by Douglas of the Roc family of four air-launched missiles that were extremely advanced for their day. The weapons were similar in appearance, with a distinctive circular wing that ringed the torpedo-shaped fuselage like a large donut. They differed primarily in their guidance systems.

The VB-10 Roc II, which appeared in 1943, was similar but used a television guidance system. It was one of the first weapons to successfully exploit the emerging technology of television for guidance systems. Such work was then being done at RCA, which had acquired the patents of Hungarian inventor Kalman Tihanyi, an early pioneer in the field of practical television applications. The Roc family was eventually expanded to include such weapons as the infrared-guided VB-11 Roc III and the VB-13 Roc IV, which was guided visually by a weapons-system operator.

Gargoyle

The Germans led the world in most phases of missile development throughout World War II with weapons such as the Hs.293 and the Bv.143, but there were several interesting and little-known American projects. These included the Navy's ASM-N-2 Bat and ASM-N-4 Dove air-to-surface missiles developed by an in-house government effort headed by the Bureau of Standards and the Navy Bureau of Ordnance in close collaboration with the Massachusetts Institute of Technology. One of the most promising projects, however, was the McDonnell LBD-1 (later KSD-1) Gargoyle glide bomb, which was ordered in 1943. It was a true precursor to the GBU series of weapons that would later emerge during the Vietnam War, and which were still being developed for use in both Gulf Wars decades later.

Parallel development of similar projects often took place, and, in the case of the U.S. Navy, parallel designation systems for glide bomb programs evolved, as secret projects were cubbyholed to keep them away from prying eyes in other departments. This is why the Gargoyle was not designated under the joint-service ASM system, but under the U.S. Navy's LB (later KS), for bomb-carrying glider, nomenclature.

The Gargoyle anti-ship missile had the distinction of being the first missile built by the McDonnell Aircraft Company. Though it was an insignificant maker of airplane parts during World War II, the St. Louis–based company would eventually evolve (as a component of the McDonnell Douglas Corporation) into the largest maker of military aircraft in the United States and the originator of the Harpoon anti-ship missile.

The LBD-1 was a swept-wing, butterfly-tailed missile ten feet one inch long, with a wingspan of eight feet six inches. It weighed 517 pounds empty but carried twice its own weight—1,000 pounds—in explosives. It was first flown in March 1944 with a small rocket engine attached. Beginning in December of that year, a series of tests demonstrated that when dropped from twenty-seven thousand feet, it had a range of five miles. The guidance system was in development when the war ended, and little is known

The Gargoyle was America's answer to German weapons like the Henschel Hs 293 and the legendary Fritz X weapon that got everyone's attention when it was used to sink the British cruiser HMS *Spartan* and several other vessels off Salerno in 1943. *McDonnell Douglas*

about the Gargoyle as it receded back into its secret and mysterious cubbyhole at the dawn of the Cold War.

Katydid

As McDonnell was developing the Gargoyle as an offensive weapon, it also produced the Katydid, a pulsejet-powered target drone. The U.S. Navy initiated the project in 1942, assigning the designation XTD2D-1 to a series of prototypes. The production-series vehicles were designated as TD2D-1 during World War II, and as KDH-1 after 1946. The Katydids had a wingspan of twelve feet two inches, and were eleven feet two inches long. They cruised at roughly 250 miles per hour and had an endurance of about forty minutes. The basic configuration of the Katydid was adopted for that of the Kingfisher offensive missile.

Kingfisher and Puffin

A direct descendant of the Gargoyle and Katydid was the Kingfisher family of anti-ship missiles, developed by the National Bureau of Standards and produced by McDonnell. Like the previous missiles, they had the distinctive V tail, and visually they were very similar to the Katydid. Indeed, both the Katydids and Kingfishers were powered by jet engines, while the Gargoyle was rocket propelled. As with the Gargoyle, the Kingfisher carried a 1,000-pound warhead. Unlike the rocket-propelled Gargoyle, the Katydid and Kingfisher had McDonnell pulsejet engines. The Kingfisher had a range of twenty miles and a top speed of Mach 0.7.

When the XAUM-6 Kingfisher Model F was first introduced, the U.S. Navy considered arming various aircraft with the weapon, from the carrier-based AD-2 Skyraider to the long-range PB4Y-2 Privateer patrol plane and the P5M-1 Mariner flying boat. Late in the missile's development, McDonnell even proposed that the U.S. Air Force consider arming B-47 and B-50 strategic bombers with them. In each case, they would have been carried on underwing pylons, rather than in the internal bomb bays.

An XAUM-6 Kingfisher is seen here at the McDonnell factory in St. Louis, mounted on the underwing pylon of a Douglas JD-1. The JD-1 was a variation on the U.S. Army Air Forces' A-26 Invader that was used by the U.S. Navy for testing missiles and target drones. *McDonnell Douglas*

The airframe of the Katydid pulsejet-powered missile clearly had a lot in common with that of the Gargoyle. The McDonnell Aircraft Company produced both missiles. *McDonnell Douglas*

Here we see the main fuselage of an XAUM-6 Kingfisher on the factory floor at St. Louis. Without its wings and engine, it looks a lot like a torpedo. *McDonnell Douglas*

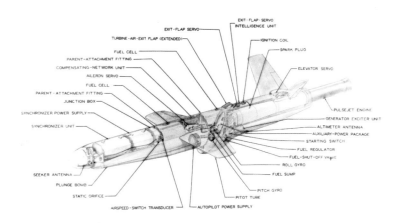

This cutaway drawing clearly illustrates the inner workings of the XAUM-1 Kingfisher. Though this is 1940s technology, in many ways it is similar to modern anti-ship missiles, such as the Harpoon. *McDonnell Douglas*

In September 1947, the Kingfisher F was renamed Puffin, and the following year, the designation was changed from AUM-6 to AUM-N-6 to confirm that it was a navy weapon. It was tested by the navy though 1949, but was apparently never used in combat. Two decades later, McDonnell would merge with Douglas, and from McDonnell Douglas would come the AGM-84 Harpoon, the ultimate turn-of-the-century air-launched anti-ship missile.

Gorgon

As the McDonnell family of guided missiles was in development, the U.S. Navy's Naval Air Development Center (NADC) turned to the Glenn Martin Company in 1943 to aid them in developing another family of air-launched guided missiles. It was named Gorgon, after the daughters of Ceto and Phorcus of Greek mythology. These girls, Spheno, Euryale, and Medusa, were known collectively as Gorgons because of their snake-infested hair.

Just as there were several Gorgons in mythology, there were several Gorgons developed at the naval aircraft factory at Philadelphia and produced by Martin. After building the early Gorgons itself, the navy turned to private industry.

As with the McDonnell family, a variety of propulsion systems were used for the Gorgons. The first one, the turbojet-powered KUN-1 Gorgon I, evolved into the rocket-propelled NU2N-1 and the CTV-N Gorgon II subfamily, which included the CTV-N-4 Gorgon IIC, which was intended to be surface launched. The Gorgon IIC weighed just under a ton, had an eleven-foot wingspan and was eighteen feet long. It was similar in design to the German Fiesler Fi.103, better known as the infamous V-1 cruise missile. Both the U.S. Navy and the U.S. Army Air Forces had tested the V-1 and had built reverse-engineered copies known as Loons. The Gorgon IIC differed from the V-1 in that it had a set of forward, or canard, wings in addition to its main wings. Later Gorgons differed further by having the engine mounted below, rather than above, the fuselage.

A Gorgon IV is mounted on the underwing pylon of a Northrop P-61 Black Widow night fighter. Though this was just for testing purposes, it suggests that the U.S. Army Air Forces had an interest in using Gorgons for night operations. *Martin Marietta*

In the late 1940s, the U.S. Navy seriously considered arming Convair PB4Y-2 Privateer patrol planes with a brace of operational AUM-N-6 Puffins for operations against Soviet shipping. *Author's collection*

Facilities for the ramjet-powered Gorgon IV's flight-test operations, circa the 1940s, were relatively Spartan at this remote location in the far west of the United States. *Martin Marietta*

During the spring of 1945, as the U.S. Navy was gearing up for the massive amphibious invasion of the Japanese home islands of Kyushu and Hokkaido, the Gorgon IIC played an important role in their tactical planning. The plan was to launch them from both escort carriers and landing craft. They had a range of up to ninety miles and a cruising speed of around four hundred miles per hour. A substantial planned production run was terminated when the war ended in September without the invasion.

After World War II, Martin built, and the U.S. Navy tested, a small number of ramjet-powered Gorgon IVs, which were air-launched weapons. No Gorgons are known to have been used in combat, and the program was terminated in 1953.

Aphrodite and Anvil

Secret, strange, and deadly are all words that describe the weapons code-named Aphrodite and Anvil. They were the ultimate American flying bombs of World War II, and their deployment provides one of the most tragic footnotes in the story of America's most trouble-plagued political dynasties.

The story of World War II flying bombs, the precursors of today's cruise missiles, could easily fill an entire volume. The Germans led the way with the Fiesler Fi.103, which Adolf Hitler personally nicknamed the V-1, or vengeance weapon. The U.S. Army Air Forces experimented with a series of crude cruise missiles, as well as with the notion of remotely piloted conventional aircraft packed with explosives.

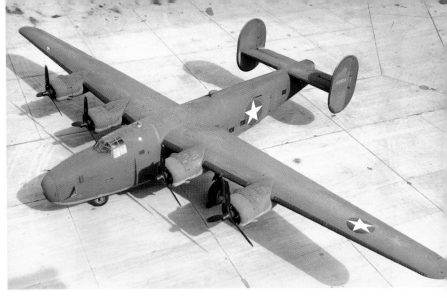

It was in 1944, with smaller aircraft having been rejected as ineffective, that both the U.S. Army Air Forces and U.S. Navy jointly decided to turn full-size heavy bombers into flying bombs. These weapons were secret then, and they remain so secret that even today few details of their operations are common knowledge. They are known to have been used in the European theater and are believed to have been intended for use in the Pacific. Roughly twenty-five to twenty-seven Boeing B-17F and B-17G Flying Fortress heavy bombers were field-modified in England and redesignated as BQ-7 under the U.S. Army Air Forces' Project Aphrodite. Meanwhile, at least two (but possibly more) Consolidated Liberators were also converted and redesignated as BQ-8. Designated B-24 by the U.S. Army Air Forces and PB4Y-1 by the U.S. Navy, the Liberators had a longer range and a slightly greater payload capacity than the Fortresses. The Liberators were converted under a program known as Project Anvil, which is not to be confused with Operation Anvil, the original name for the August 1944 Allied invasion of southern France. (After it was planned, but before it occurred, this operation was renamed Dragoon by Winston Churchill.)

The two known BQ-8s were former U.S. Navy PB4Y-1s, and were flown by the Navy's VB-110 bomb squadron based at Blythburgh, England. Their gun turrets were removed, and the flight decks were reconfigured as open cockpits to permit an easy escape for the pilot and copilot. The ten-man crew was cut to just the two. The aircraft were then packed with twenty-five thousand pounds of impact-fused Torpex explosives. The Anvil's payload gave it

This photograph provides a good idea of what the BQ-4 Project Anvil flying bomb looked like. Because it was so secret, no pictures are known to have been taken of the mysterious craft. However, it was essentially an unarmed B-24 Liberator strategic bomber, and so was the C-87 long-range transport, which is the aircraft pictured here. Lieutenant Joseph Patrick Kennedy, the son of the former United States ambassador to the United Kingdom and the older brother of John F. Kennedy, was killed flying the first BQ-4 mission in 1944. *Author's collection*

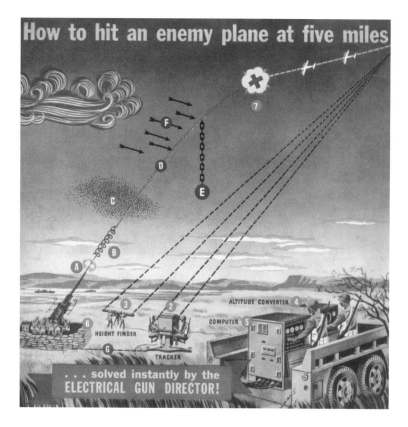

How to hit an enemy plane at five miles

... solved instantly by the
ELECTRICAL GUN DIRECTOR!

This illustration explains graphically how a 1944 computerized electrical gun director calculated the trajectory by which the 90mm anti-aircraft battery would take out a high-flying Focke-Wulf Fw 200. The bomber (1) is spotted and followed by the tracker (2) and height finder (3), which feed information into the altitude converter (4) and the computer (5). The computer plots the plane's distance, course, and speed, aims the gun (6), and sets the fuse of the shell to burst at a calculated point (7) for a hit. This computer, or "electrical brain," calculates the muzzle velocity of gun (A), shell drift to the right due to its spin (B), air density (C), time of shell's flight (D), the downward pull of gravity (E), direction and velocity of wind (F), and even the distance between tracker and gun (G). *Author's collection*

the biggest non-nuclear punch of any guided missile in history.

The BQ-8s could be radio controlled after a human crew got them airborne, with a ground-based controller "flying" them through the use of a television camera in the nose that sent back real-time imagery of where the aircraft was headed. In this sense, they were operated like the MQ-1 Predator pilotless aircraft that were seen as technological marvels when they were operated over Afghanistan more than a half century later. Because the range of the television signal was so short, however, the operator was shifted from the ground to an accompanying aircraft.

Aphrodite and Anvil operations were reserved for high-priority targets that were heavily defended and hardened. These included German V-1, V-2, and V-3 sites in France that were protected by many feet of reinforced concrete. At least eight BQ-7s were expended in actual missions, as were the two known BQ-8s.

The initial Anvil mission was flown on August 12, 1944. The target is believed to have been one of Germany's strangest secret weapons, the V-3 Hochdruckpumpe (HDP, or high-pressure pump), a massive multi-chambered 150-mm gun, 490 feet long, with a range

of more than one hundred miles. The V-3 site was at Mimoyecques, near Calais, France. The pilot was U.S. Navy Lieutenant Joseph Patrick Kennedy, the son of the former United States ambassador to the United Kingdom and the older brother of John F. Kennedy, the future American president. Reportedly, Elliot Roosevelt, the son of President Franklin D. Roosevelt, was present that day aboard one of the accompanying aircraft. Apparently, when Kennedy set the fuses in preparation for abandoning the BQ-8, they misfired, and the Torpex exploded in midair.* On September 3, 1944, the second BQ-8 mission successfully obliterated a hardened German base in Heligoland.

Computer Technology and the Electrical Gun Director

It is now generally forgotten that electronic computing for military applications was truly born in World War II. The technology was crude by twenty-first-century standards, but systems such as the electrical gun director introduced by Western Electric, circa 1944, were scarcely inferior to many systems that were commonly seen in the military inventory in the 1960s. The vacuum-tube systems born in World War II would remain state of the art until the widespread application of transistor technology.

Indeed, during World War II, computers were already being called computers, although they were often referred to with great hyperbole as electrical brains. This is how the general public could comprehend this bewildering technology that once had been unthinkable.

Western Electric, the manufacturing division of Bell Telephone, was a leader in communications and electronic technology, and it would remain so for more than a generation after World War II. The company tackled the problem of calculating how to hit an enemy bomber flying at sixteen thousand feet and at a range of five miles, which was within the range of a 90-mm anti-aircraft battery. A shell would take perhaps twenty seconds to reach it, but in the meantime the aircraft would have flown nearly two miles. The electrical gun director would be able to tell the gun where to aim to hit such a speeding target.

*One year and one day later, on August 13, 1945, the Navy posthumously awarded Kennedy its highest award for valor, the Navy Cross.

Project X-Ray

Perhaps the strangest of the strange weapons that were built and tested during World War II was that which was developed under the almost comically mysterious code name Project X-Ray. The story is so strange as to seem like the sort of science fiction suggested by its pulp-fiction code name, but it was not.

Shortly after the United States entered the war, an Irwin, Pennsylvania, dentist, Lytle "Doc" Adams, theorized that bats could be used to destroy Japanese cities. Adams hypothesized that small incendiary devices could be attached to thousands of these small flying mammals, which could then be released by American bombers over Japan. Because bats are known to take up residence in the eaves of wooden buildings, they would naturally position themselves—along with the attached miniature fire bombs—in places where they could do the most damage. Adams imagined that a timer or temperature sensor could trigger the incendiary after the bat was in position. Each bat would give its life for the American war effort, and thousands of fires would erupt across Japan.

Because of the long distances in the Pacific theater, it was not until late 1944, when the Boeing B-29 became operational and bases in the Marianas Islands became available, that routine bombing missions against Japanese cities finally began. The early missions involved high-explosive ordnance. It was not until early 1945 that General Curtis LeMay's Twentieth Air Force switched from high explosives to incendiaries. What LeMay figured out in 1945, Doc Adams had understood in 1941: Most Japanese housing construction was wood and paper, so incendiaries were a far more effective weapon than high explosives.

As Albert Einstein had been able to get his secret memo about nuclear weapons onto the desk of President Franklin Roosevelt in 1939, so too did Adams manage to get the ear of the president. After reviewing the proposal, Roosevelt ordered the U.S. Army Air Forces and the National Defense Research Committee to initiate a development program. In passing Adams' hypotheses along to General William J. "Wild Bill" Donovan, head of the Office of Strategic Services (OSS), the president added a postscript to the order, penciling in the phrase that would warm the heart of any eccentric inventor: "This man is not a nut."

Bats were collected at Carlsbad Caverns in New Mexico and Bracken Cave near San Antonio, Texas. Initial testing began in 1943 under the auspices of the U.S. Army Air Forces at Muroc Army Air Field (now Edwards Air Force Base) in California's Mojave Desert. As testing got underway at Muroc in 1943, a number of problems arose. One of the primary issues was how to carry the bats and release them from the bomb casings without injuring or killing them. For example, it was discovered that the bats did not do well in the cold temperatures at high altitudes. Those that didn't freeze to death were too groggy to escape from the casing and fly away. When they were carried at lower altitudes, it was hard for the bats to get out of the falling bombs, even when the bombs were slowed with parachutes.

When the bugs were worked out of these predicaments, and the bats were successfully deployed, they proved to be unpredictable. For testing, a series of target buildings was constructed for the bats to attack. However, some of the bats flew into the wrong buildings. The incendiaries went off, burning down unintended structures, as

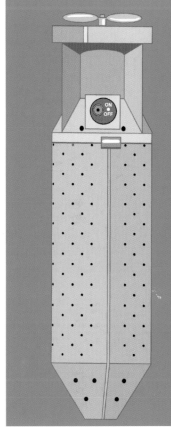

The legendary bat bomb of Project X-Ray was about the same size as a conventional five-hundred-pound high-explosive bomb. There was a parachute in the upper section, and a stabilization propeller at the top. Inside the main shroud were five circular egg-crate trays, each containing individual compartments for thirty-one bats in rows of 5-7-7-7-5. When the parachute deployed, the main shroud dropped away and the confused bats scattered. *Bill Yenne illustration*

This tank for dispensing poison gas at low altitudes was designed to be fitted on U.S. Army Air Forces attack aircraft. Had it ever been used, the pilot would have simply released the valve, letting the slipstream serve to spread the noxious fumes.
Author's collection

well as the intended target buildings. A general's staff car was also destroyed by the bats.

Under the code name Project X-Ray, the program was transferred to the U.S. Navy. The so-called bat bombs were scheduled to become operational early in 1944, but when the project was delayed, it was reportedly cancelled. However, this writer has spoken with a navy transport pilot who flew a squeaking cargo to the western Pacific around this time. When he asked what the sound was, he was told by the cargo handlers that it was bats, but that he was not to ask any more questions.

The story of this strangest of the strange weapons is told in detail in *Bat Bomb: World War II's Other Secret Weapon*, by Jack Couffer, a member of the team that developed the bat bomb.

Low-Level Poison-Gas Dispenser

There were a number of reasons why poison gas was never used in World War II, outside of China. When the war began, all of the major combatant nations had stockpiles of various types of poison gases that were loaded in shells or canisters and ready for use. The horrible memories of the gas's deadly effects in World War I were certainly part of the reason why it wasn't used. Indeed, Adolf Hitler himself had been gassed and severely injured on August 13, 1918, near Ypres, Belgium.

In 1925, the Geneva Protocol for the Prohibition of the Use in War of Asphyxiating, Poisonous or Other Gases, and of Bacteriological Methods of Warfare was adopted. It prohibited only the use of poison gas in warfare, not its manufacture. Between 1932 and 1937, unsuccessful attempts were made to work out an agreement that would

also prohibit the production and stockpiling of biological and chemical weapons.

Featured here is one of the weapons from the American arsenal. It was a spray device that was about the same size and shape as an aircraft's external fuel tank. A pair of these would have been mounted on two underwing pylons, and the gas would be released at very low level, much as a crop duster releases his chemicals on crops. The gas would have to be released at very low levels in order to ensure a lethal concentration.

The United States also began the war with a stockpile of bombs containing mustard gas. These agents were placed into bomb cases that were the same sizes as standard thirty-pound and one-hundred-pound high-explosive bombs. These delivery systems would have been preferable to spray, because a higher concentration could be delivered and because mustard gas is a so-called persistent gas that does not dissipate as fast as agents such as chlorine and phosgene.

It is commonly assumed that chemicals were not used because of the threat of retaliation in kind. While this may have been a factor, available documents also show that military staffs on both sides were skeptical about the utility of chemical weapons and did not recommend their use. Of course, each side knew that the other had generally good anti-chemical protection.

Field Telephones

During World War II, radio communications were revolutionized by the Handy-Talkies and Walkie-Talkies discussed in the following entry, but the preponderance of battlefield communications still relied on land-lines. During World War I, the U.S. Army Signal Corps had created an enormous telephone system, but this was dwarfed by what was done in World War II. Indeed, it is easy to imagine that in many areas of action in World War II, the U.S. Army operated a larger intact telephone system than was available to the indigenous population. The men who strung the thousands of miles of field wire, often under fire and under the same battlefield conditions being experienced by the infantry, are among the great unsung heroes of World War II.

The cornerstone of the U.S. Army land-line communications system was the EE-8 family of portable field telephones. They operated on dry-cell batteries and were used at the platoon, company, and battalion level, and even higher in front-line situations. The range was typically about a dozen miles or more, depending upon how much line had been run and its condition.

The EE-8s were carried in a case that was 9.5 inches on its longest dimension, and weighed just under ten pounds. Initially, the case was made of leather, but this material didn't hold up so well, especially in the humidity of the Pacific theater, and later production models were equipped with a canvas bag. All of the controls and terminal points were located on the top of the unit for easy operation.

Networks of EE-8s were connected through various types of switchboards. The early systems included the four-line BD-9, dozen-line BD-11, and the large forty-line BD-14. Later in the war, the more sophisticated BD-71 and BD-72 became more common. The six-line BD-71 was portable but weighed between forty-five and nearly sixty pounds. The twelve-line BD-72 weighed as much as eighty pounds. One each of the BD-71 and BD-72 could be combined into an eighteen-line system, but

The high command studies the map of the Italian beachhead area, while the colonel relays information to the general. The colonel is communicating by way of a an EE-8 portable field telephone. *Author's collection*

because of cord lengths, two BD-72s apparently could not be linked.

Among the many later systems, the BD-89 switchboard had twenty magneto-line circuits and thirty-seven common manual-line circuits for corps headquarters use, and was incorporated into a TC-2 telephone exchange. The BD-110 had ninety lines and as many as a half dozen of these could be linked to form a telephone exchange. At a higher level were TC-1 or TC-10 telephone exchanges with one hundred to three hundred line capacity that were used at the army headquarters level.

Handie-Talkies

Many items of equipment used by U.S. troops in World War II are overlooked from today's vantage point because they now seem so ordinary. Many of these—including handheld communications devices—were quite revolutionary at the time. When it seems like everyone has a cellular telephone today, it's difficult to remember a time when handheld communications devices didn't exist.

The idea of handheld communications for American troops was the brainchild of Paul Galvin, whose Galvin Manufacturing Company of Chicago originated the brand name Motorola. When told about the cumbersome inconvenience that troops experienced with heavy backpack

During World War II, field telephone communications passed through a variety of portable switchboards. The six-line BD-71 and the similar twelve-line BD-72 were among the most common by 1944, although earlier BD-11s were still to be seen. *Author's collection*

"Handie Talkie"

★ Pioneered and developed exclusively by Motorola Electronics Engineers, this mighty, little 2-Way Radio is fighting for final Victory on every major battle front.

ANOTHER Motorola Radio 1st

For production "beyond expectation" Motorola has received its third award. It is the aim of every Motorola employee to produce faster and better until final Victory has been won.

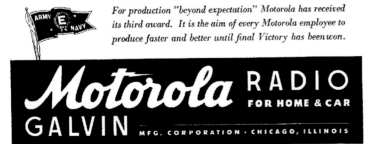

ARMY E NAVY

The Motorola SCR-536 Handie-Talkie revolutionized personal communications for the infantry on the battlefronts of World War II. They and their cousin, the Walkie-Talkie, were also vital for behind-the-lines commando activities. *Author's collection*

radios, Galvin sent his chief engineer, Don Mitchell, to observe the 1940 maneuvers in Wisconsin. Mitchell reported back to Galvin, and work began on developing a lighter, simpler two-way radio that was truly man portable.

The result was the amazing self-contained SCR-536 Handie-Talkie, which was about a foot long (with antenna retracted), weighed six pounds, and had a range of a mile or more. It was waterproof and could even survive being submerged. The SCR-536 entered production in the summer of 1941, and about one hundred thirty thousand units were eventually built.

The SCR-536 was followed by the more compact SCR-300 Walkie-Talkie, which had the capability to deliver clear communications through intense background noise. Galvin manufactured about fifty thousand SCR-300s, and large numbers of these were available to U.S. troops during the Italian campaign and to those who landed in Europe with Operation Overlord on June 6, 1944. They proved their worth in the European theater and are recognized as having been one of the key items of infantry equipment during the confusion that ensued during the Battle of the Bulge in December 1944. Walkie-Talkies were also widely used in the later battles of the Pacific theater and in the Korean War.

Essentially, the Handie-Talkie and Walkie-Talkie revolutionized the way that American soldiers operated, making it hard to imagine a day when instantaneous handheld communications didn't exist.

Noise-Suppressing Miniature Radio Receivers

One of the key issues in battlefield voice communications is audibility. Even if there is a clear link via radio or field telephone, can the voice on the receiver be heard over the roar inside a tank, the confusion of a beachhead, or the din of an artillery barrage? To address this issue, the U.S. Army Signal Corps contracted with the Sonotone Corporation of Elmsford, New York, in 1942 to address the problem. A major producer of civilian hearing aids, Sonotone developed what it called midget receivers. Working with the Signal Corps technical staff, Sonotone created a new headset that was reduced in size to fit under the army's 1942-model M1 battle helmet, which would become ubiquitous during World War II and remain essentially unchanged for four decades. A key technological feature of the Sonotone products was the miniaturized vacuum tubes. Had transistors existed, things would have been much easier.

Manufactured at Sonotone's facility in White Plains, New York, the midget receivers are said to have worked under any climatic conditions from a New Guinea jungle to a Kiska fog. By the summer of 1944, roughly five hundred thousand of the headsets were in service with United States forces worldwide.

Ghosts with Rubber Guns

They were invasion craft that didn't exist, loaded with weapons that were never forged, and pointed for attacks that were never planned. This was the equipment that appeared and disappeared overnight in harbors along the English channel, helping to confuse the Germans in the hectic days preceding D-day on June 6, 1944.

One of the most celebrated classes of secret gadgets of World War II involves an arsenal of

The tiny Sonotone midget receivers are seen here against an image of the cacophonous battlefield action that made them necessary. *Author's*

harmless pneumatic-rubber weapons that was manufactured for a ghost army. In advance of Operation Overlord, the massive Allied cross-channel invasion of France from England in 1944, deception was essential. The Germans knew that the invasion was coming. That fact could not be hidden. What the Allies could hope to do was to keep the enemy guessing about the when and where of the invasion.

The obvious place for an invasion was the Pas de Calais region, where the English Channel is narrowest. On a clear day, the Germans in Calais could easily see the white cliffs of Dover. German planners were divided over whether the invasion would come at the easiest crossing point. The actual invasion would take place east of the Cotentin Peninsula in Normandy, but the Allies had to convince the Germans to reinforce Calais. The entire northern coast of France was fortified with the Atlantic wall, which consisted of millions of tons of steel and concrete with fixed gun emplacements. But there were not enough mobile reinforcements to back the entire line. To fool the enemy, the Allies created the First U.S. Army Group (FUSAG), and they went so far as to name the general the Germans feared most— George S. Patton, Jr.—to command it. However, FUSAG did not exist.

To create the illusion of the existence of FUSAG, the U.S. Army created a complete ghost army, the nucleus of which was the 23rd Head-quarters Special Troops, an organization that included artists, designers, actors, meteorologists, and sound technicians, whose mission

Uninflated rubber dummy equipment, plus a compressor to do the inflating, have been prepositioned on a beach by U.S. Army engineers. The army secretly deployed inflatable light and medium tanks, 90mm anti-aircraft guns, 155mm guns, landing craft, and other large weapons to deceive the enemy.
U.S. Rubber Company

Under the watchful eyes of U.S. Navy and U.S. Army officers, a group of sailors unpack inflatable gear on the shore of the English Channel. *U.S. Rubber Company*

This is the first step in launching the inflatable rubber equipment used so successfully by the army engineers to fool the Germans in several important European operations during World War II. In this photo, men are laying the rubber ground cloth on which the vehicles such as dummy tanks and artillery would be assembled. *U.S. Rubber Company*

was simply to spoof the Germans. In the months leading up to the June 6 invasion, they burned up the airwaves with a massive volume of communications among the myriad—albeit nonexistent—components of the phony FUSAG. This radio traffic was actually a huge and ongoing radio play created for the Germans to intercept.

The ghost army also had an enormous arsenal of weapons, including M3 light tanks, M4 Sherman medium tanks, 90mm antiaircraft guns, 155mm field guns, transport vehicles, and landing craft. These were lightly camouflaged and parked throughout southeast England, where German reconnaissance aircraft detected them. Unfortunately for the Germans, all of these weapons were collapsible pneumatic rubber decoys.

The rubber tanks and landing craft were manufactured by companies such as Goodyear Tire & Rubber, Firestone, and the United States Rubber Company (later Uniroyal) using the types of rubberized fabric then being used for the manufacture of large barrage balloons and rubber rafts. One of the most important manufacturing

Decoy equipment such as this rubber landing craft (seen here against the backdrop of the English Channel with crews checking the inflatable floor), as well as tanks and guns, were easy to send to combat areas because they were collapsible and packed compactly. They could be inflated quickly in the field, and deflated easily for moving to a new location. *U.S. Rubber Company*

centers was the United States Rubber Company's Alice Mill on Fairmount Street in Woonsocket, Rhode Island. Beginning in 1943, thousands of rubber decoy weapons were manufactured and shipped overseas to England.

Thanks to this rubber ruse, the illusion of the phantom FUSAG succeeded. When the invasion troops landed in Normandy, most Germans in places of higher authority, including Adolf Hitler, thought that it was merely a diversion. Hitler ordered that the Panzer divisions

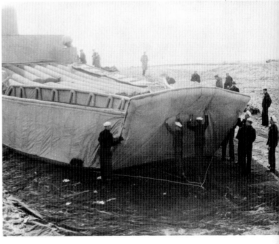

One of the phantom fleet is being readied for action along the English Channel. What looked like PT boats, landing craft, and barges were actually pneumatic, balloon-fabric, full-scale models that were produced under top-secret, high-priority contracts. *U.S. Army*

These sailors are launching a decoy rubber landing craft at the shore of the English Channel. This collapsible, pneumatic craft was part of the Ghost Army developed and operated by army engineers to fool the Germans. *U.S. Rubber Company*

needed in Normandy be kept near Calais to repulse the "real" invasion. By the time that the Germans realized that Normandy was the real invasion, the Allies already had an inextricable foothold.

The 23rd Headquarters Special Troops transported their rubber tanks to the continent and went on to participate in operations across France and into Germany, where their 1,200 officers and men repeatedly impersonated units ten times their size or larger. The information about the rubber hardware was released to the public in December 1945, but the details of the full war of deception would remain secret for more than half a century.

A Gas Bag to Keep Gas Out

Poison gas, one of the most terrible weapons of the First World War, was not used in combat in World War II, except by the Japanese against the Chinese, mainly in Manchuria. Nevertheless, when the war began, there was a fear, and

indeed an expectation, that gas would become a weapon once more. In the United States, as in Britain, gas masks were issued to troops, and they were made available to civilians in case the enemy launched gas attacks on cities.

In addition to gas masks, systems for sealing buildings and other protective measures were developed for the bleakest scenario. One of the most interesting means of protection against poison-gas attack was the gasproof tent. The U.S. Army developed it, but it would probably have been available to civilians as well.

The gasproof tent could be folded down and packaged in a small box, but in the event of a gas attack, it could be folded out to contain enough volume for one person to crawl in and wait for the all-clear. Of course, one of the major problems with this system was that a person would probably be breathing rather heavily from the anxiety of being under attack, and as such, the oxygen within the airtight enclosure would probably have been exhausted in about an hour. But many of the most dangerous poison gases, including chlorine and phosgene, are highly volatile and dissipate within about ten minutes. Mustard gas, however, is much more persistent.

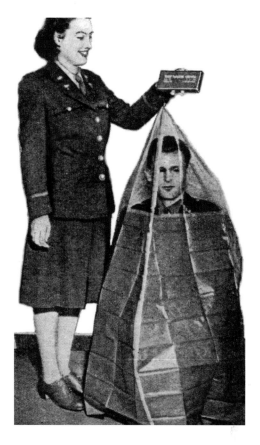

Launching a decoy rubber landing craft (at right), with a real landing craft for comparison in the foreground. *U.S. Rubber Company*

This young WAC has not simply bagged a man, she has bagged him in an airtight gasproof tent. She holds the box into which this compact protective device would fit. He seems none too pleased, although he would have had the last laugh if there had been a gas attack. *U.S. Army*

Blackout Glasses

During World War II, whether you were in a combat zone or at home in a city that was susceptible to possible enemy air attack, nighttime was blackout time. As had been painfully demonstrated during the Battle of Britain in 1940, enemy bombers could use the lights of everything from theater marquees to street lamps to farmhouses to locate the targets for their bombs. Every home was fitted with black curtains, and outdoor lighting was switched off for the duration.

Against this backdrop, however, people had to get around at night, and they had to see what they were doing. Limited lighting was permitted, but it was still hard to see outside. To address this problem, New York City optometrist Dr. Maxwell Miller developed his unique blackout glasses. Designed for both military and civilian defense applications, they gave individuals a personal light source. A tiny electric bulb was fitted to each frame and shielded to keep direct light out of the wearer's eyes. The power source was a small pocket-sized battery pack. The light shield also directed the beams of light downward, so the lights were not visible from above.

Portable Airplane Detector

During 1941 and 1942, the possibility of German and Japanese air attacks against the United States was a constant fear. This had happened to the cities of Europe and Asia, and there was no reason to think that it would not happen to the United States. U.S. Army Air Forces interceptors stood ready, as did army antiaircraft guns, but civilians did not want to stand by helpless. They trained themselves to scan the sky and recognize enemy aircraft. Air-raid wardens were appointed, and they organized civilian defense at every level. The need for this had been made evident in Britain, and Americans lost no time in following suit.

By the summer of 1942, a unique portable airplane detector was made available to civil defense personnel. A parabolic concentrator picked up the sounds of approaching aircraft and filtered out extraneous sounds. The operator would simply turn until the sound was the loudest, and would thus be facing in the direction of the approaching aircraft. A carrying case contained an amplifier, batteries, and other equipment. These self-contained units turned individuals everywhere into mobile listening stations.

Sperry Gyroscopic Fire Control

World War II was probably the last war in hundreds of years of naval history in which there were battles between large warships on the high seas. American warships achieved such superiority that this kind of warfare became obsolete. Excepting aircraft carriers, nowhere did surface warship technology more clearly reach its peak than in the great battleships of the U.S. Navy. A key reason for the success of these powerful vessels was fire control. The three triple turrets of sixteen-inch guns could lay down withering fire, but fire control was the key to the guns realizing their deadly precision.

Hitting an enemy ship miles away, from a rolling, pitching warship, involved complex challenges, which were answered by the technological wonder of electronic fire control. A

With a parabolic concentrator on her head, this young civil defense spotter is ready to locate the sounds of approaching aircraft. She'll use her binoculars to identify them. If they are from an enemy nation, the authorities will soon know.
Author's collection

She might use Dr. Miller's Blackout Glasses for civil defense duties, or merely to read a book on the train, but for a soldier in the field, the doctor's prescription might make the difference in whether or not a jammed weapon got back into service expeditiously.
Author's collection

In this 1943 advertisement, the Sperry Corporation described its unique fire-control systems, then in use on U.S. Navy warships. The company attributed the United States Navy's high accuracy and speed of gunfire to its products. *Author's collection*

generation before any precursor of the modern computer was available for shipboard use, the Sperry Corporation developed a fire-control system to calculate the angle of a gun, elevation, lead, and other factors to achieve pinpoint accuracy.

The company was formed by Elmer Sperry, who began his career as an entrepreneur while studying electrical engineering at Cornell University, when he invented the nationally acclaimed electromagnetic regulator. He founded the Sperry Gyroscope Company in 1910 to manufacture and market his marine gyrostabilizing devices, which were used by the U.S. Navy in World War I. Sperry and his firm were years ahead of their time, and the American armed forces beat a path to his door. Indeed, the company soon came to be known as the "brain mill for the military." Sperry passed away in 1930, but his son Lawrence carried on his work, making Sperry a world leader in electronics when that field was little understood outside the scientific and technical community.

Rotating Barrel Anti-paratroop Weapon

The world looked on in horror at newsreels of German airborne troops sweeping into civilian areas from Holland to Norway in 1940. Even before the United States entered the war, the fear of this scene repeating itself on this side of the Atlantic led to the development of countermeasures. Shooting down the transport aircraft carrying the enemy troops would have been one solution, but something was needed to engage the airborne troops after they had left the aircraft. Shotguns and rifles were a solution, but here we highlight a unique multibarreled weapon that was rolled out for United States civilian defense applications in late 1940.

Handmade by Civil Defense volunteers and field tested at New York's Floyd Bennett Field, this twelve-barrel (manually advanced) single-shot rotary gun could fire a variety of rounds, and dissimilar ammunition could be placed in the various

Battleship X sinks an enemy ship *18 MILES AWAY!*

How was this done? What made it possible?

To hit an enemy ship miles away, from a rolling, pitching warship, involves complex problems, the *complete* answers to which are known only by our naval personnel and by a small group of companies specializing in such problems.

Here are a few of the factors which enter into the solution of these problems:

1. Direction and speed of enemy ship.
2. Direction and speed of our ship.
3. Distance to enemy ship.
4. Time required for shell to travel to enemy.

Furthermore, the shell travels in a curve, its true course being affected by many things, such as:

5. The rotation of the earth.
6. Direction and velocity of wind.
7. Weight, shape, and velocity of shell.

The answer, which takes into account *these and other problems*, must be available *immediately*, since both our ship and the enemy ship are on the move.

Our Navy must *know* where the enemy ship will be when our shells arrive, many seconds or even a minute after leaving the guns. And to get our shells to arrive at this precise spot, the angle of gun elevation, lead, and all other factors must be calculated with unbelievable accuracy, and the gun put into correct firing position.

The present mechanical marvel, called *fire control*, which solves these problems, involves among other things the use of hydraulics, optics, calculating machines, and electronics. Naturally, it did not spring into being overnight.

It is the result of years of inventive development by companies like Sperry, co-operating fully with and receiving full co-operation from the Armed Forces.

Since it takes so many years to perfect such equipment, the development work, engineering, and testing had to be completed during peacetime.

Otherwise there would have been no equipment ready when war came.

All this took large sums of money and the best efforts of highly trained, specialized engineers.

In addition to the development of many peacetime devices, Sperry companies have specialized in the creation and manufacture of fire-control equipment for the Navy since 1908.

The United States Navy leads the world in accuracy and speed of gunfire.

BACK THE ATTACK BUY WAR BONDS **SPERRY CORPORATION** 30 ROCKEFELLER PLAZA, NEW YORK 20

FORD INSTRUMENT COMPANY, INC. SPERRY GYROSCOPE COMPANY, INC. VICKERS, INC. Waterbury Tool Division. VICKERS, INC.

113

A technician demonstrates the twelve 37mm rotating barrels of this unique anti-paratroop gun at Floyd Bennett Field, on Long Island, in 1940. An enemy paratrooper descending on New York City might have faced certain death when this weapon was turned skyward. *Author's collection*

This young doctor with the U.S. Army Medical Corps is thankful to have plasma for her patients at a front-line field hospital. *Author's collection*

barrels simultaneously. Among the rounds that could be adapted for the gun's 37-mm barrel were high explosives, smoke shells, one-pound fragmentation bombs, and even parachute flares.

Plasma Transfusion Technology

Just as World War II saw the birth of widespread military applications of computer and electronics technology, so too did it mark a revolution in medical technology, especially with respect to United States forces. This led to an incalculable increase in the number of American lives saved on worldwide battlefields, and the United States emerged from World War II as a world leader in medical technology.

Few commodities are more vital to saving the lives of battlefield casualties than blood. Blood transfusions had become routine early in the twentieth century, but whole blood is fragile and has a shelf life of just a few days. In the late 1930s, however, Dr. Charles Drew, a New York mass-transfusion specialist, discovered that whole blood could be replaced for transfusion purposes by plasma, the liquid part of blood in which red and white blood cells and platelets are in suspension. Whole blood is more than half plasma, and plasma is

mostly water, making it durable and transportable. This made possible the widespread collection of blood in the United States, from which plasma could be extracted and shipped overseas to the troops.

During World War II, the American Red Cross converted more than ten million units of blood into plasma and made it available for troops overseas. The lives saved were countless, but probably in the hundreds of thousands.

Penicillin

The antibiotic that revolutionized the treatment of infection saw its first widespread use among American forces in World War II. As with plasma, penicillin was first widely available on the battlefields of that war, and it is credited with saving hundreds of thousands of lives. The antibiotic properties of the Penicillium chrysogenum (formerly Penicillium notatum) mold were discovered by Ernest Duchesne in 1896, forgotten, and rediscovered by Alexander Fleming in 1928. However, it was not until late in the 1930s that serious field trials revealed the astonishing potential of penicillin.

In 1941, the U.S. government requested that the American pharmaceutical industry undertake a major effort to figure out a way to mass produce what was referred to as a wonder drug. Late in 1942, after many discouraging false starts, Jasper Kane at Pfizer developed a fermentation process

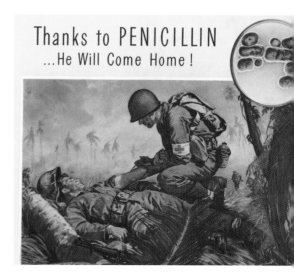

A dish of mold spores hardly seems to be a likely candidate for one of the most important items of military equipment in World War II, but the lives saved were incalculable. *Author's collection*

Two small but revolutionary technological innovations are found in this 1942 advertisement. The sulfanilamide in the tiny package was certainly a vital item, but so was the packaging. Cellophane's ability to keep the sulfanilamide safe and fresh was essential to its potential to save lives. *Author's collection*

that was the needed mass-production break-through. Though Pfizer shared its technique with other companies because of the wartime urgency, the company went on to produce the lion's share of the millions of doses of penicillin that went overseas with the troops during World War II.

Sulfanilamide

In combat medicine, it is axiomatic that the earlier a patient is treated, the better his chances of survival. To achieve this, it is necessary to bring the treatment as close to the soldier as possible. In World War II, no item of a soldier, marine, or airman's personal gear was more important to medical treatment than sulfa drugs. The infantryman carried sulfanilamide in a small satchel attached to his belt. When dusted onto an open wound, it would prevent infection in the critical minutes before a combat medic could reach the man.

Of course, sulfanilamide was also an important part of the gear that the medic carried with his equipment, and it was an essential step in treating the injured before they could be transported to a field hospital. Sulfa drugs were also important in the treatment of bacterial diseases such as pneumonia and meningitis.

Iwan Ries Telescope

One of the satisfying things that we find in the social history of World War II is the number of small companies that stepped up to provide civilians and individual GIs with useful gear at reasonable prices. One such piece of equipment was the handy five-power Iwan Ries telescope that was marketed for just half a dollar, postpaid. That's about ten dollars in today's valuation, but still reasonable.

The telescope came with a free identification chart showing the profiles of enemy aircraft that one might expect—or fear—in the airspace over the United States. This company is probably unrelated to the famous Chicago tobacconists, Iwan Ries and Company, which dates to 1857.

The Iwan Ries Telescope was marketed in this advertisement that features an illustration of a uniformed air-raid warden. The silhouettes at the bottom are of a Messerschmitt Bf 109 and a Junkers Ju 87. Both of these aircraft had been used against civilian populations in Britain and throughout continental Europe. *Author's collection*

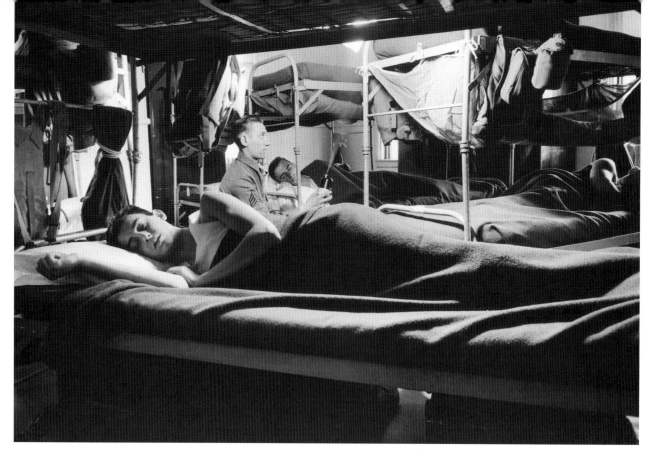

In World War II, mosquitoes were our enemy and DDT was our friend. In this April 1943 photograph, Sergeant Edward Haladay uses an aerosol spray can inside his barracks while his comrades are asleep. According to the Department of Agriculture, he released enough "insecticide smoke" to kill any insects lurking in the barracks. The accompanying statement from the USDA stated, "The aerosol will not harm the sleeping soldiers nor will it take fire from any unprotected flame." Mosquitoes are still not our friends. *USDA photo by Knell*

By June 1943, when this picture was taken, DDT was already being used by GIs in the Mediterranean theater to eliminate malaria-carrying insects. Sprayed into the pup tents of soldiers camped in mosquito-infected areas, the aerosol insecticide killed any mosquitoes in the tent. The batting kept out any others, and the soldier inside was spared the mosquito bites that might be dangerous, and surely uncomfortable. The footwear is hardly field issue. *USDA photo by Knell*

Aerosol Dichloro-diphenyl-trichloroethane (DDT)

The history of warfare, and indeed the history of everyday life, is punctuated by tales of "miracle" products that solve one problem only to create others. Such was the case of the use of mercury to cure ailments such as syphilis. It worked, but mercury poisoning was ultimately lethal. Another such product is dichloro-diphenyl-trichloroethane (DDT). It eliminated the dreaded disease malaria from much of the world, but it entered the food chain with debilitating results.

It was long understood that mosquitoes carry the parasite that causes malaria, a disease that enters the liver and blood cells and attacks the body's immune system. When the United States entered World War II, it was apparent that American service personnel would be fighting in areas where mosquitoes and cases of malaria, as well as other insect-borne diseases such as typhus, were common, if not rampant.

Laboratory tests of DDT and other chemical insecticide agents had been ongoing, and in 1943 the U.S. Department of Agriculture reported the effectiveness of DDT in killing lice, which spread typhus, and the remarkable success of DDT against mosquito larvae. Production during 1943 was limited to louse powder, because other noncritical materials were available as effective larvicides. However, the National Research Council Conference on Insecticides and Repellents recommended the use of DDT in an aerosol spray, and by the spring of 1944 it was available for mosquito control in malarious areas.

The first studies of airplane application of DDT to kill mosquitoes were conducted during the fall of 1943, and by April 1944 the U.S. Army Air Forces were conducting field trials in Panama. The spraying of DDT oil solution over jungle forest at the rate of 0.4 pounds of DDT per acre reduced the number of adult mosquitoes by more than 90 percent and killed practically all mosquito larvae. On the basis of those favorable results, airplane spraying projects were carried out in all the theaters where mosquito-borne diseases were problematic.

In Italy, DDT operations were carried out in the vicinity of Naples, Rome, and in the Arno Valley from Livorno to Florence, as well as around the U.S. Army Air Forces bases in the Foggia region. The result was a virtual eradication of malaria and other insect-borne maladies. This was a boon to United States troops, as well as Italian civilians. Malaria essentially disappeared from Europe as a result of the American effort.

After World War II, DDT was used extensively as an agricultural insecticide, but increasing evidence began to show that it was concentrated in the food chain and potentially hazardous to humans. Most notable among its detrimental effects was its causing certain bird species to lay eggs with thin shells. A major decline in the bald eagle population was attributed to DDT. This led to curtailment of its use and eventually to its being banned in most of the industrialized world during the 1970s.

Hull Streamline Compass

There was big equipment, and then there was the ubiquitous small gear that was essential to U.S. operations during World War II. One such gadget was the streamline compass from the Hull Manufacturing Company in Warren, Ohio. The term streamline refers to the styling of the compass case, which had to remind the GIs of gadgets they remembered lying around the house back home.

As ordinary as it seemed, the compass would prove vital as American soldiers, marines, and airmen made forays into unfamiliar territory amid the sandstorms of North Africa, the jungles of New Guinea, and the blizzards of northern Europe.

The Hull compasses from the 1940s were extraordinarily durable. Many have survived and are still available through collectors and on eBay. The original military-issue compasses are prized by military vehicle collectors. A vintage jeep needs a vintage Hull compass.

The Hull Streamline Compass was in service with the vehicles of the U.S. Army during World War II, and it was also available to civilians, stocks permitting. These compasses are still prized by collectors. *Author's collection*

CHAPTER THREE
THE COLD WAR

The desperate times of the Cold War led to desperate measures, and to weapons and devices of desperation. Many such items beg the rhetorical question, "What were they thinking?" These were weapons of last resort that illustrate how dreaded the overwhelming Soviet ground superiority in Central Europe was in the 1950s. Among these weapons, some of the most improbable include those with which we begin this chapter.

While on the ground the Cold War spawned desperate measures, at the opposite extreme, outer space offered promise. The space race between the Soviet Union and the United States to put people into space and on the moon was certainly a theater of the Cold War, but here the conflict was more bombast than bombs, and the weapons were designed for voyages of discovery rather than offensive action.

An exception was the Soviet R-36-O fractional orbital bombardment system (FOBS) that would have involved ICBMs launched southward from the Soviet Union, traveling through outer space across the South Pole and approaching the United States from the south.

Theoretically, FOBS could be "parked" in orbit, where it could hang over the United States like Damocles' sword.

FOBS notwithstanding, neither side really wanted to fight World War III in outer space; they eventually agreed to ban offensive weapons in space through the Outer Space Treaty (Treaty on Principles Governing the Activities of States in the Exploration and Use of Outer Space, Including the Moon and Other Celestial Bodies), signed on January 27, 1967, and entered into force on October 10, 1967.

As soon as they were able, however, both sides quickly began development of a series of surveillance, or spy, satellites. The series developed by each side was in service and routinely scanning the territory of the other by the 1960s, and successors to the early spy satellites are still in orbit today.

Though offensive weapons in space were banned, defensive weapons were not. In the 1980s, the United States began to consider building a defense against Soviet ICBMs, and one of the basing modes under consideration was outer space. Space-based ballistic-missile

Above: Symbolizing the dawn of the computer age at the Lawrence Livermore National Laboratory, where America designed its fast-growing nuclear arsenal, is this UNIVAC computer console and IBM equipment in October 1956. Lawrence Livermore accepted delivery of its first computer, a UNIVAC, in 1952, the year of the laboratory's founding. *Lawrence Livermore National Laboratory*

Opposite page: A Martin Marietta Aero & Naval Systems technician demonstrates a fiber-optic hose connector, circa 1989. *Martin Marietta*

Computer operators at Lawrence Livermore National Laboratory work at IBM 650 computer consoles, circa October 1956. Lawrence Livermore accepted delivery of its first IBM computer in 1954. By the late 1950s, the laboratory was working on a variety of supersecret gadgetry other than nuclear weapons. *Lawrence Livermore National Laboratory*

defense was one of many scenarios that were explored under the Strategic Defense Initiative (SDI) initiated by Present Ronald Reagan in 1983. Because the objective of SDI was to create a means of destroying Soviet warheads in space at the apogee of their trajectory, SDI came to be known in the media as "Star Wars." Although SDI did not actually envision fighting wars in outer space, the euphemism—tied to a popular series of movies—stuck.

The decision to proceed with SDI played a key role in bringing about the collapse of the Soviet Union and the end of the Cold War. SDI plays a key role in the final pages of this chapter, but ahead of that are many of the other, more conventional, systems that were developed and deployed by the United States armed forces during the Cold War.

The Atomic Cannon

The M65 atomic cannon was the product of a desire on the part of the U.S. Army to develop a self-contained nuclear-strike capability at a time when the U.S. Air Force managed and controlled most of the U.S. offensive nuclear arsenal. With a maximum range of nineteen miles, or as little as seven miles with a Mk.9 nuclear shell, this bat-

tlefield weapon would have left its crew dangerously close to a nuclear detonation.

The U.S. Army had studied the feasibility of a mobile 240-mm gun during World War II, when troops came under fire from the very large artillery employed by the Germans, especially at Anzio. By the late 1940s, these studies had evolved to the point where work began on the creation of a gun capable of firing a nuclear shell. The atomic cannon program began in 1950 with the specifications increased to 280mm. The result would be the largest mobile gun ever deployed by the U.S. Army, and certainly the most deadly. A total of twenty of the weapons were manufactured at the Watervliet Arsenal in Watervliet, New York. The first of them was completed in early 1952, and tests were conducted with conventional shells through the first part of 1953.

Now it was time to test the real thing. The M65 test program was incorporated into the U.S. Army's Operation Upshot Knothole, a series of eleven tests of battlefield nuclear weapons that were conducted between March 17 and June 4, 1953, at the Atomic Energy Commission's Nevada Test Site. The actual nuclear weapons involved were developed by the Los Alamos Nuclear Laboratory. Upshot Knothole was, in turn, conducted in conjunction with Desert Rock V, a readiness exercise designed to train troops to fight on a nuclear battlefield. An estimated twenty-one thousand military personnel were involved in the operation.

The Upshot Knothole tests, of which films are still widely shown to illustrate the effects of nuclear blasts, included detonations of weapons mounted on towers or dropped from aircraft. They ranged from the nuclear equivalent of two hundred tons of TNT to forty-three kilotons. The tenth test, or shot, was code-named Grable, and it was to be the only live firing by the M65. This test occurred on May 25, 1953, at Frenchman Flat, on the Nevada test site. Fired a distance of just seven miles, the Mk.9 shell delivered a fifteen-megaton blast. This detonation, with its five-hundred-foot mushroom cloud, was observed from a distance of less than ten miles by seven hundred observers, including Secretary of Defense Charles Wilson and Chairman of the Joint Chiefs of Staff Admiral Arthur Radford, as well as 2,600 troops. According to the U.S. Army,

The first and only live firing of the U.S. Army's atomic cannon occurred at 8:30 on the morning of May 25, 1953, under the code name Test Shot Grable. The 280-mm shell with its fifteen-megaton warhead was hurled seven miles. Hundreds of high-ranking armed forces officers and even members of congress were present. *National Archives*

some of the soldiers approached to less than a half mile of ground zero soon thereafter.

Grable was the only M65 nuclear test, but it was deemed successful, and the guns were ordered into production. Beginning in late 1953, the first of between ten and sixteen atomic cannons were deployed overseas to Europe, and one nuclear artillery battalion was formed, the 3rd Battalion of the 82nd Artillery. Attached to V Corps of the 3rd Armored Division, they were tasked with counterattacking a Soviet armored invasion of West Germany. Annual test firings of the weapons—with conventional rounds, of course—are said to have been conducted at Grafenwohr.

Atomic cannons were mobile guns, transported either by road or rail on a rail chassis constructed by the Baldwin Locomotive Works. The gun itself had a 38.5-foot barrel and weighed forty-seven tons, while the entire transporter unit weighed in at eighty-three tons. In 1955, the lighter Mk.19 round, which offered a range of fifteen to eighteen miles, was introduced. By 1957, the M65 battalion in Europe was operational with the new shell, but six years later, the U.S. Army withdrew the atomic cannon from service and disbanded the 3rd Battalion.

The atomic cannon is today generally forgotten, but not gone. Surviving examples, albeit now inoperable, can be seen at the Yuma Proving Ground near Yuma, Arizona; the Rock Island Arsenal at Rock Island, Illinois; the Army Ordnance Museum in Aberdeen, Maryland; the Atomic Museum in Albuquerque, New Mexico; the Fort Sill Museum in Oklahoma; the Virginia War Memorial Museum in Newport News; and the Watervliet Arsenal. Another is also on public display on a hilltop near Junction City, Kansas, overlooking Interstate 70 and the U.S. Army's Fort Riley.

Davy Crockett

Like the atomic cannon, the Davy Crockett was a Cold War nuclear weapon designed to be used by small units in the field to equalize the enormous Soviet numeric advantage in troops and tanks. With the atomic cannon, the blast radius of the warhead came dangerously close to exceeding the range of the gun. With the Davy Crockett, well, the use of these weapons would have been essentially suicidal.

The weapon was named for the famous nineteenth-century congressman turned soldier of fortune whose life and heroic death at the Alamo in San Antonio were memorialized in a series of Walt Disney films in the 1950s. The Davy Crockett gave U.S. Army infantry units as small as a platoon a nuclear capability. Known

A large number of somber-faced guests gathered at the Baldwin Locomotive Works in May 1953 to observe a demonstration of the M65 atomic cannon and its intricate gun carriage mechanism.
Author's collection

The Davy Crockett, seen here in March 1961 at the Aberdeen Proving Ground in Maryland, was the smallest nuclear weapon delivery system ever deployed by U.S. armed forces. With a range of less than three miles under the best circumstances, it was fire and forget—forget the gunner, that is! *Author's collection*

informally as the nuclear bazooka, the Davy Crockett could be fired from two recoilless rifles: the M28, an adaptation of a 120-mm recoilless rifle, and the M29, analogous to the larger 155-mm recoilless rifle. The M28 weighed just over one-hundred pounds, could be carried by a jeep, and fired the Davy Crockett's M388 nuclear projectile to a range of 1.5 miles. The M29 had a range of 3 miles; it weighed nearly four hundred pounds but could be carried by a variety of medium-sized vehicles, including two-and-a-half-ton (deuce-and-a-half) trucks. More than six thousand of the M28 and M29 rifles were believed to have been ordered by the U.S. Army, although the number of M388 nuclear rounds is thought to have been closer to four hundred.

The Davy Crocketts were deployed overseas to Germany with the 3rd Armored Division from 1961 through 1971. The weapons system was involved in two live-fire nuclear tests. Designated as Little Feller 1 and 2, these were conducted in Nevada during July 1962.

Eventually, U.S. Army brass was said to have become concerned about having a nuclear weapon that was under the command of platoon sergeants. The potential for misuse in the fog of battle was considered to outweigh the potential usefulness of the weapon. Like the atomic cannon,

the Davy Crockett was withdrawn from service, but only after having been deployed for a decade.

Lobber

The Convair Lobber must rank as one of the strangest of Cold War weapons. There were many missiles that were similar to it, but the contents of its warhead were unique. The history of American missile systems during the 1950s is characterized by the rapid pace of development of missiles of all sizes and shapes and with varying sizes of conventional and nuclear warheads. All branches of the armed forces got into the act, and there was a clear rivalry going on between them. What is little known is that the army's Quartermaster Corps was one of the players in the rivalry, and that they envisioned using a missile to transport supplies!

The idea was that the Lobber could literally lob supplies to troops that were surrounded and needed supplies, such as ammunition. The U.S. Army had previously used artillery shells to deliver supplies, notably during the siege of Mortain, France, in August 1944, so the use of a missile was not that much of a leap of the imagination.

Seen here during U.S. Army field testing in December 1958, the Convair Lobber looks like an offensive weapon, but it was actually designed to carry supplies. *Author's collection*

A soldier sights the Convair Lobber launch tube as two of his comrades assemble the Lobber missile itself. The Lobber could hurl fifty pounds of supplies about eight miles. *Author's collection*

In 1958, the U.S. Army commissioned the Convair Division of General Dynamics to build the missile. Convair brought to the project the experience of having developed the U.S. Navy's RIM-2 Terrier surface-to-air missile and the U.S. Air Force's SM-65 (later PGM-16) Atlas. The Terrier was one of the first great shipboard guided missiles of the postwar period, and the Atlas was America's first operational intercontinental ballistic missile (ICBM).

Convair built a simple nine-foot-long solid-fuel rocket that had a top speed of 1,500 miles per hour. The fifty pounds of supplies that were packed into the Lobber's nose cone were delivered by parachute, although there was a shock absorber in the nose. The payload could be delivered up to a distance of eight miles, but the accuracy was apparently never fully fine tuned. Being solid fueled, the Lobber's engine could not be throttled, so it would simply fly until the fuel burned.

The results of the flight testing encouraged Convair to suggest other payload possibilities, including high explosives, napalm, and chemical weapons. Even nuclear weapons were suggested for the little Lobber. The missile shone brightly in the pantheon of weapons from which the U.S.

The three segments of the Convair Lobber supply missile were the nose cone, the supply canister, and the engine section. The missile and its launcher were designed to be carried and operated by a three-man team, but an additional man was present during U.S. Army field tests in December 1958. *Author's collection*

The U.S. Marine Corps tested the Convair Lobber on the beach at Camp Pendleton, California, in January 1959. The Lobber was about nine feet long and had a ten-inch diameter. *Author's collection*

Army could choose during the urgent days of the Cold War, but its moment in the limelight was fleeting, and the Lobber eventually faded into obscurity.

Project Y and the Avrocar

The myths and legends suggesting that the U.S. government has been secretly testing flying saucers obtained from beings from other worlds ebb and flow in popularity. The first peak in the popularity of such tales came in the 1950s, not long after the term flying saucer was coined in 1947 by private pilot Kenneth Arnold, who thought he saw such aircraft in the vicinity of Mount Rainier in Washington.

Hollywood was keen to make us believe they were from outer space, but a corollary to this myth holds that the disc-shaped aircraft seen in the 1940s and 1950s had actually originated in wartime Germany. An often repeated, but never confirmed, legend holds that a disc-shaped, gyroscopically stabilized German aircraft exceeded the sound barrier in a test flight near Prague in February 1945. Dates for the test flight vary depending on which account one reads, but most fall within the first three weeks of February. The February 1989 issue of the German

periodical Flugzeug contains what is alleged to be an eyewitness account of a person who saw disc-shaped aircraft at Praha-Kbely airport (Prag-Gbell in German) near Prague.

No evidence of either extraterrestrial or German flying saucers has ever been authenticated, nor has any experiment with disc-shaped aircraft ever been confirmed. However, in the 1950s, the U.S. Army did in fact test a disc-shaped hovering vehicle. The VZ-9-AV Avrocar was the very embodiment of the Hollywood image of what a flying saucer should look like. It was a silvery metal disc eighteen feet in diameter with two bubble canopies for the crewmembers. Unlike the Hollywood saucers of the 1950s, the Avrocar was real. Not only that, it was nurtured with the research-and-development funding of at least two national governments.

Originally designated with the fictional-sounding code name Project Y, the Avrocar originated with the Avro-Canada Company in 1952. At that time, the Canadian government was anxious to encourage a world-class aviation industry in Canada, and such advanced projects as Project Y were part of it. It was to be a disc-shaped supersonic aircraft that could be used as a high-altitude fighter or an attack aircraft. Project Y was

One of the strangest craft of the 1950s, the Avro VZ-9-AV Avrocar looked like the embodiment of that era's image of a flying saucer, but reportedly it could barely get off the ground, and it had a forward speed of less than forty miles per hour. The project was cancelled in 1961. *U.S. Air Force*

to possess a vertical takeoff and landing (VTOL) capability though the use of a powerful engine in the center of the disc, which directed its thrust straight down.

The Avro-Canada engineers almost certainly had access to information by way of the British intelligence services that a similar design had emerged from the drafting tables at Focke-Wulf during World War II. The Focke-Wulf aircraft was slightly elliptical in order to accommodate a vertical stabilizer at the rear, but the Avro vehicle had no vertical surfaces of any kind, and it was destined to be perfectly circular.

The propulsion concept was similar in the two aircraft. In the center of the Focke-Wulf, there were two huge contra-rotating propellers that turned parallel to the ground. The propeller blades were thus the lifting surface, like the rotors of a helicopter. Because the props turned in opposite directions, their torque would be balanced and the aircraft would be quite stable. The Project Y vehicle would be jet propelled, with jet exhaust radiated to the edges of the machine and redirected downward by means of a series of valves.

The Canadian government abandoned Project Y within two years, but it was picked up by the U.S. Air Force, where it would be developed

under the designation VZ-9-AV. The VZ stood for VTOL Research, while the AV stood for the manufacturer. The fact that it was the ninth in the series of VTOL research vehicles indicated how serious the Americans took the quest for vertical flight. Two prototypes were completed in 1959, although flight testing did not take place until 1961.

When it was discovered that the VZ-9-AV could barely get off the ground and would not be able to operate at high altitude, the U.S. Army evaluated it as a hovercraft to carry troops across swamps. It was here that the nickname Avrocar was coined as being more appropriate. The flying saucer was more of a skimming saucer, with a top speed said to be less than forty miles per hour, making it slower than an army truck. Helicopters were more practical for flying troops over swamps. The project was cancelled in 1961.

Perhaps just as strange as the Avrocar itself is the fact that both prototypes still survive. One is at the U.S. Army Transportation Museum at Fort Eustis, Virginia, and the other is at the Smithsonian's Paul Garber facility at Silver Hill in Maryland. Conspiracy theorists still maintain that the Avrocar was a cover for other German-derived discs that actually did fly high into the stratosphere.

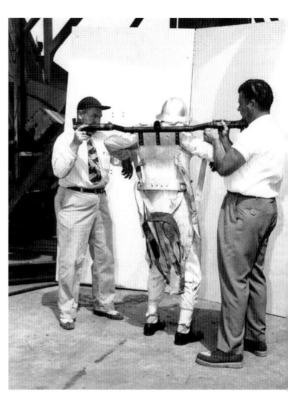

The harness system for the small rocket lift device is strapped to the back of a test pilot at the Redstone Arsenal. The hard hat was considered necessary in case of a malfunction, but it may not have been adequate protection. *Redstone Arsenal*

Jet Vest

A technician at the U.S. Army's Redstone Arsenal demonstrates the small rocket lift device, also known as the jet vest. He seems confident that it will work. *Redstone Arsenal*

Invented by Thomas Moore at the U.S. Army's Redstone Arsenal near Huntsville, Alabama, the small rocket lift device was one of several personal propulsion systems developed during the late 1950s and early 1960s. Also known as the jet vest or lift belt, it was strapped to an individual to enable him to hop over terrain features such as small gullies or rivers and land upright. Its tanks contained pressurized nitrogen and hydrogen peroxide fuel. Small nozzles pointed down, emitting a high-pressure stream of gas. Pitch and roll were controlled by body movements.

Initial tests conducted in June 1961 demonstrated that the jet vest was safe and reliable enough to proceed with manned flight testing. However, the amount of gas that could be carried limited the total flight time to twenty seconds, which was considered inadequate for operational use, and the concept faded away.

Poised for takeoff, this man is ready for a tethered test of the Redstone small rocket lift device. *Redstone Arsenal*

USS *Desert Ship*

Located within the thirty-two thousand square miles of the U.S. Army's White Sands Missile Range in New Mexico is a U.S. Navy ship. Not simply a navy installation, the site is commissioned as a landlocked U.S. Navy ship, the USS *Desert Ship.* Designated as LLS-1, the vessel is also known as White Sands Launch Complex 35. During the 1950s, the U.S. Naval Air Warfare Center used the complex for testing of shipboard missiles such as the Talos surface-to-air missile (pictured below).

During the 1980s, the Ballistic Missile Defense Organization used the facility, and the High Energy Laser Systems Test Facility was used for programs such as MIRACL (mid-infrared advanced chemical laser) and the SEALITE beam director—a U.S. Navy program from the 1980s that was designed to demonstrate whether a lethal laser could be adapted as a defense system for ships. The SEALITE beam director—a prototype of a shipboard laser turret—consisted of a large gimbaled telescope with a 6-foot aperture and optics to be used to point the MIRACL beam onto a target. USS *Desert Ship* is still used to test naval surface-weapon systems. The U.S. Navy has one other landlocked ship, the USS *Rancocas*, an Aegis missile testing facility near Moorestown, New Jersey, that is known locally as the "cruiser in the cornfield."

Stored-energy Circuit Breakers

There were several firsts with the launch of the navy's USS *Glacier* (AGB-4) in 1955. She was the navy's first icebreaker in the decade since World War II, and she was outfitted with equipment from the ITE (inverse time element) Circuit Breaker Company, an innovator in the electrical industry and the creator of the first stored-energy low- and medium-voltage circuit breakers. ITE was also the first to create five-kilovolt air magnetic circuit breakers.

The rotating-disc inverse time element is a tripping mechanism for use in overload and circuit protection. In a typical electro-mechanical relay, there are two elements, a clapper or solenoid type, and an induction inverse time element type. In solid-state relays, three of each may be combined into a single relay unit. The timing process of an inverse time element begins as the disc rotates in an electromechanical relay. The time dial is then set, adjusting the time delay curve. The setting is governed by the desired current value to avoid overheating.

ITE was named for its revolutionary oil-dash-pot inverse time element for electro-mechanical circuit-breaker-trip devices. The firm was later acquired by Siemens Energy & Automation, a subsidiary of Germany's Siemens AG, but the ITE name is still well known to those involved in the electronics field.

Launched in 1955, the navy icebreaker USS *Glacier* (AGB-4) in 1955 was equipped by ITE, the maker of the first stored-energy low- and medium-voltage circuit breakers. *Author's collection*

News of electrical progress from I-T-E

U.S.S. "GLACIER," AGB-4, Length 310 ft. Beam 74 ft. Displacement 8300 tons. Builder, Ingalls Shipbuilding Co.

Navy's New Icebreaker Uses I-T-E Electrical Control and Distribution Equipment

First icebreaker launched for the Navy since World War II, the *U.S.S. Glacier* is the prototype for an entirely new class. Much of the *Glacier's* duty will be performed while she is plowing alone through vast fields of ice. Her equipment must be dependable—able to take the rough, bruising shocks to which she will be exposed. I-T-E switchgear has proven itself in rugged marine applications for over 44 years. I-T-E Circuit Breaker Company, 19th & Hamilton Sts., Phila. 30, Pa.

I-T-E SWITCHGEAR is used for ship's service, emergency and distribution circuit protection. Illustrated is an emergency Generator and Distribution Switchboard.

I-T-E

I-T-E CIRCUIT BREAKER COMPANY, Philadelphia, Pa. • Greensburg, Pa. • Victor, N.Y.
BullDog Electric Products Company, Detroit, Mich. • BullDog Electric Products Company (Canada) Ltd., Toronto • Eastern Power Devices Ltd., Toronto, Canada

Meanwhile, the USS *Glacier* had her shakedown cruise as part of the Operation Deep Freeze I mission to Antarctica, during which she broke ice to provide an open channel into the offloading site for the establishment of the Naval Air Station at McMurdo Sound. She led Operation Deep Freeze II and participated in Deep Freeze III during the International Geophysical Year of 1957–1958. She was involved in continuous operations off McMurdo Station through 1965, being retired by the navy in 1966 after eleven Deep Freeze operations.

Nuclear Falcon

The strange concept of very-short-range nuclear weapons was not the sole purview of the U.S. Army during the dark and desperate days of the Cold War. The U.S. Air Force also produced such a weapon. As with the army's atomic cannon and nuclear artillery, the basic idea was to go nuclear in order to offset Soviet numeric advantages.

During the 1950s, the principal challenge faced by the U.S. Air Force's Air Defense Command and the joint U.S.–Canadian North American Air Defense Command (NORAD) was defending North American air space from overwhelming numbers of Soviet long-range bombers. Interceptors armed with conventional weapons could certainly shoot down some, or perhaps most, of the bombers. However, each

one that got through would put a mushroom cloud over a United States or Canadian city.

One proposed solution for countering the masses of Soviet bombers was to fight nuclear fire with nuclear fire. A nuclear weapon detonated within a bomber formation would create a fireball that would destroy them all—or most of them—and create a shock wave that would wipe any stragglers from the sky. Such a weapon was the AIM-26 nuclear Falcon.

The precursor to the AIM-26 nuclear Falcon was the AIM-4 Falcon air-intercept missile. Development of the original Falcon began in 1946 with the Hughes Aircraft Company, one of two aircraft companies started by the eccentric billionaire Howard Robard Hughes, Jr. The other company was the aircraft division of his tool company, which built his various airplanes (such as the H-1 Racer, D-2 and XF-11 spyplanes, and his huge H-4 Spruce Goose), and which evolved into the Hughes Helicopter Company. The Hughes Aircraft Company, meanwhile, built no aircraft but became a leading manufacturer of guided missiles.

The Hughes Falcon carried various designations, including the F-98 fighter, but Falcons entered service with the U.S. Air Force as the GAR-1 through GAR-4 (GAR stood for guided aerial rockets) and became the AIM-4 family in 1962. Through the years, tens of thousands of Falcons were built, ranging in length from 6.6 to 7 feet and packed explosive payloads of nearly thirty pounds. They were powered by Thiokol solid-fuel rocket engines, and the ultimate Falcon, the AIM-4G (originally GAR-4A), had a top speed of Mach 4 and a range of seven miles.

It was in 1956, as the Falcon was becoming standard equipment with the F-89s and F-102 interceptors of the Air Defense Command, that thoughts turned to using a nuclear warhead for the missile, and the Nuclear Falcon was ordered. Initially, studies were done for an XGAR-5 with radar homing guidance and an XGAR-6 with infrared homing, but neither project reached the hardware stage. In 1959, work began on the XGAR-11, and the operational GAR-11 started equipping F-102 units in 1961.

The nuclear Falcon was designated the AIM-26 in 1962. The missiles were seven feet long, with a two-foot wingspan and a diameter of eleven-inches. They were powered by Thiokol M60 solid-fuel rocket engines and had a top speed of about Mach 2 and a range of up to ten miles with a W54 quarter-kiloton nuclear warhead.

During the 1960s, the Raytheon AIM-7 Sparrow gradually replaced the AIM-4 Falcon, but there was no nuclear Sparrow. The AIM-26 remained in service with the U.S. Air Force until the early 1970s. By that time, the doctrine for bomber operations on both sides of the Iron Curtain had shifted from high-altitude to low below-radar penetration. For a U.S. interceptor to fire a nuclear weapon from above against a low-flying plane over American territory was considered unacceptably destructive, and the AIM-26 was finally phased out.

Zuni

Aerial rockets used as large-diameter, long-range projectiles became commonly used armament for combat aircraft during World War II. They were primarily employed as a ground-attack weapon, but the German Luftwaffe interceptors routinely employed them against Allied-bomber formations.

After World War II, and until guided missiles became practical and widely available, the U.S. Navy and the U.S. Air Force continued to develop high-velocity aircraft rockets (HVAR) and folding-fin aircraft rockets (FFAR). The folding fins allowed the latter rockets to fit into tubes in multiple-round launchers. Well-known types included the 2.75-inch Mighty Mouse FFAR and the 5-inch Holy Moses HVAR. The Mighty Mouse was launched from nineteen-round tube launchers and used an air-to-air weapon. Just one hit from a barrage could down an enemy aircraft. Used as an air-to-ground weapon, the Holy Moses remained in production until 1955.

The five-inch Mk.16 Zuni FFAR was developed at the Naval Ordnance Test Station at NAS China Lake in California during the 1950s as the successor to the Holy Moses, and operational Zunis began entering service in 1957. They were used on a variety of aircraft with a variety of warhead options, including both point detonation and delayed action. They would be used mainly, albeit not exclusively, for air-to-ground missions.

Introduced in 1971 was the Mk.16 Zuni's successor, the Mk.71 Zuni wraparound-fin aerial rocket (WAFAR). With a diameter of 130 mil-

limeters, or slightly more than five inches, it is generally the same length as the Mk.16 Zuni, although lengths vary according to warhead. The Mk.16 had a range of about three miles, the Mk.71 nearly twice that distance. Both were powered by small, solid-fuel rocket engines. The Mk.71 Zuni is still in the arsenal today, typically launched from the LAU-10 family of launchers.

Redeye

The name should have been infra-redeye because it is derived from the infrared homing system used by the General Dynamics FIM-43 Redeye. The weapon was the first man-portable air defense system (MANPADS) fielded by United States forces, and it was used by both the U.S. Army and the U.S. Marine Corps.

Convair F-102 test pilot Robert G. Laurence and a friend pose with a Hughes GAR-2 (AIM-4) missile, the precursor to the AIM-26 Nuclear Falcon, at Edwards Air Force Base on December 17, 1956. The AIM-26 was a guided, nuclear-armed, air-to-air missile deployed by the U.S. Air Force. The friend holds a Zuni five-inch folding-fin aircraft rocket. *Author's collection*

General John G. Zierdt (left), commanding general of the U.S. Army Missile Command (MICOM), examines the launcher for the FIM-43 Redeye air-defense missile in June 1964. The launcher consisted of the launch tube, a gripstock, and a telescopic sight assembly with a target acquisition indicator. It had a 2.75-inch tube diameter and weighed less than twenty pounds when loaded. The gunner acquired and tracked the target through the sight, and was alerted to target lock-on by a buzzer. *Redstone Arsenal*

Reportedly, the U.S. Army had been seeking an air defense system capable of defending its troops from attacking fast jets since before the Korean War, but it was not until 1956 that studies began to focus on a lightweight system with infrared guidance. Full-scale development of the shoulder-fired missile began in 1959, but the first test firing of the Redeye missile from the Redeye launcher did not occur until 1961.

Initially, Redeye proved to be less effective than hoped, and the system was not considered operational until after 1968. Nevertheless, it would remain in the arsenal until the 1990s, and in the meantime, it was the immediate forerunner of the well-known FIM-92 Stinger shoulder-launched surface-to-air missile.

Nuclear-Powered Bombers

The United States entered the age of atomic weapons in 1945, and by the 1950s, both the United States and the Soviet Union threatened each other with bombers loaded with nuclear weapons. At the same time, nuclear propulsion was in its promising infancy, and the limits to what could be propelled by a nuclear power plant were not yet defined. Naturally, as nuclear-powered ships moved toward becoming a reality, thoughts would turn to nuclear-powered airplanes. In fact, such thoughts had filled the heads of U.S. Air Force planners before their rival service had its first nuclear-powered ships.

The U.S. Navy began laying plans for reactor-powered ships and submarines soon after World War II, and the first nuclear submarine, the USS *Nautilus* (SSN-571), would be commissioned in 1954. The upside of nuclear propulsion is essentially unlimited range. Adapted to ships, this would serve the U.S. Navy, especially its submarine service, extremely well. Meanwhile, the notion of a strategic bomber with unlimited range was the ultimate fulfillment of the doctrine of strategic air power.

The Nuclear Energy for Propulsion of Aircraft (NEPA) program was initiated in 1946, and a year later the Atomic Energy Commission, the U.S.

It never operated under nuclear propulsion, but the one-of-a-kind Convair NB-36H was the only aircraft in history to operate routinely with a functioning nuclear reactor aboard. It made forty-seven flights between September 17, 1955, and March 28, 1957, and was scheduled to be succeeded by the nuclear-powered X-6, whose airframe would have been based on that of the XB-36H. *Author's collection*

government agency responsible for the development of nuclear reactors, was created. This organization would work up the initial parameters for the design of shipboard nuclear reactors for the navy, and it would absorb the activities of NEPA as well. The commission also established the National Reactor Testing Station. It opened in 1949 at a remote inland location in the lightly populated high desert country of southern Idaho near the town of Arco.

At Arco, the commission studied the problem of whether it was theoretically possible to produce a reactor for an airplane. In 1951, it was determined that the answer, theoretically speaking, was in the affirmative. The engineering challenges would be keeping the size and weight of the reactor manageable, as well as creating designs for its radiation shield and cooling system. The nuclear reactor would require a very large airplane. Nobody had ever designed a nuclear-powered aircraft before, so the development process would be methodical, moving step by step.

The first step would be a proof-of-concept demonstrator that would be built under the designation X-6. Before that, though, it was necessary to build and fly a functioning nuclear reactor aboard a conventionally powered aircraft in order to evaluate shielding techniques. As a reactor test bed, the U.S. Air Force chose the largest aircraft in its fleet, the enormous Convair B-36 bomber. First flown in 1946, the B-36 was 162 feet long, with a wingspan of 230 feet—a larger wingspan than any other military aircraft ever in service in the United States. It was powered by six Pratt & Whitney R4360 Wasp Major piston engines with twenty-one thousand aggregate horsepower, and later models would also have four General Electric J47 turbojet engines. Even without the jets, the B-36 could take off with a quarter million pounds of gross weight and fly more than 8,000 miles. The air force ordered Convair to specially modify a B-36 test-bed aircraft under the designation NB-36H, which would simply fly under conventional power, with a functioning reactor aboard. Convair also received a contract to modify a pair of B-36s that would become the first two nuclear-powered X-6 aircraft. Late in 1951, the air force made a change in the X-6 test bed, deciding to replace the B-36 with the Convair B-60. The latter was essentially a swept-wing version of the

B-36 that was powered by eight Pratt & Whitney J57 turbojets. The first of these aircraft had already been built and was scheduled to fly in the spring of 1952.

Meanwhile in Arco, the Atomic Energy Commission undertook the construction of the first airborne nuclear reactor, designated as R-1. When the X-6s flew under nuclear power, the R-1 reactor would power the General Electric turbojet engines. The design of the propulsion system would allow the engines to transition between nuclear power and jet fuel, permitting a conventionally fueled takeoff followed by an extremely long cruise under reactor power. Nuclear cruise would easily permit a flight around the world. The total propulsion system, incorporating the reactor and engines, was originally designated as P-1, but the nuclear-powered version of the J57 turbojet would be the P-3. These changes did not affect the construction of the NB-36H.

The first flight of the NB-36H occurred on September 17, 1955, and the first top-secret flight tests of an airborne nuclear reactor were soon underway. These missions were considered so sensitive that a transport aircraft carrying paratroopers accompanied the NB-36H on every flight. Should the NB-36H have crashed or been forced to land at a civilian airport because of mechanical difficulties, it would have been the job of the paratroopers to surround the aircraft and prevent any unauthorized individuals from reaching it.

Convair's conception of the operational nuclear-powered bomber that would follow the X-6 was designated as NX-2. This artist's conception was released in July 1960. *Author's collection*

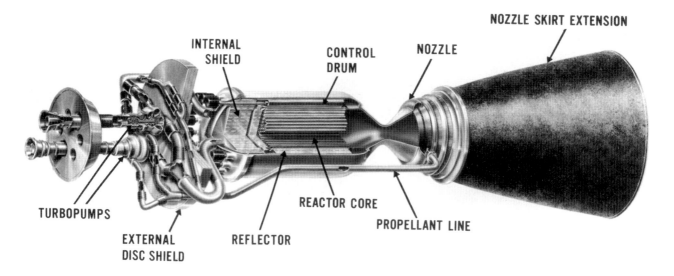

INTERNAL SHIELD

CONTROL DRUM

NOZZLE

NOZZLE SKIRT EXTENSION

TURBOPUMPS

EXTERNAL DISC SHIELD

REFLECTOR

REACTOR CORE

PROPELLANT LINE

This cutaway drawing of a NERVA thermodynamic nuclear rocket engine shows its various components. This configuration dates from 1960 and was developed by Aerojet General Corporation and Westinghouse Electric. The subsequent Aerojet and Westinghouse test series began with NERVA reactor experiment NRX-A2. *NASA*

Meanwhile, work was underway to construct a test base for the X-6 program. The NB-36H flights were conducted from Carswell Air Force Base, across the runway from the Convair factory near Fort Worth, Texas, but the air force wanted a location for the X-6 project that was farther from prying eyes. The site chosen for what was to be designated as Test Area North was near the small town of Monteview, in the Idaho desert, about forty miles northeast of the Atomic Energy Commission's National Reactor Testing Station.

An enormous hangar was constructed at Test Area North with thick lead-lined walls designed to contain radiation leakage. General Electric moved its nuclear power plant operations here and installed robotic equipment so that work could be done on the engines and reactors without exposing plant workers to excessive amounts of radiation.

The first X-6 flight was planned for 1957. The first operational nuclear bomber would, in turn, follow the X-6 in the early 1960s. The first operational wing of such aircraft was to be in service in 1964. Not only Convair, but Boeing, Douglas, and Lockheed were invited to submit proposals for the development of these bombers.

However, the incoming Eisenhower administration revisited the concept of nuclear-powered aircraft and redlined the X-6 program in 1953. The conventional B-60 program also got the ax, as the U.S. Air Force chose to acquire the Boeing B-52 instead. The NB-36H remained a live program, as did numerous feasibility studies for nuclear-powered operational aircraft for the future.

While the X-6 was not to be the first of the new breed, the concept of a nuclear-powered aircraft remained alive and well. At Test Area North in Idaho, work on the fifteen-thousand-foot runway that was planned for the X-6 program was not begun, but the other work continued. In 1955, the Atomic Energy Commission initiated a series of heat transfer reactor experiments at Test Area North's big nuclear-shielded hangar. These experiments were part of the ongoing development of airborne nuclear power plants, but the engines tested were many orders of magnitude larger than the P-1 that had been earmarked for the X-6. The idea was to refine the concept, then scale down the reactor. The goal was a thermal output of at least fifty megawatts delivered by a reactor the size of the one-megawatt reactor that would be test flown in the NB-36H. The NB-36H made its forty-seventh and last flight on March 28, 1957, having tested all phases of airborne nuclear reactor operations, from shielding to power output. In the remote Idaho desert, the heat transfer reactor experiments continued both during and after the NB-36H flight test program. A test reactor assembly designated as HTRE-1 had been built and first tested in 1955. A water-cooled uranium reactor, it weighed more than one hundred tons and was mounted on a rail car. It also demonstrated a power output in excess of twenty megawatts. Over the coming years, it was rebuilt several times. In its HTRE-3 configuration, it generated as much as thirty-five megawatts. It was also optimized for weight savings, using light aluminum structural components and hydrided zirconium as a moderator. The HTRE-3 experiments were conducted between April 1958 and December 1960, with the goal being a flight-ready hybrid turbojet-nuclear engine. Built by General Electric, this power plant reportedly would have been designated as XNJ140, with the three letters standing for experimental nuclear turbojet.

Three months after the HTRE-3 tests ended, the incoming Kennedy administration ordered the airborne nuclear propulsion program to be terminated. Secretary of Defense Robert Strange McNamara had little enthusiasm for manned bombers of any kind. He was fascinated with the potential of ICBMs and wanted the air force to pursue this line of strategic thinking. During the remainder of the twentieth century, nuclear propulsion for aircraft would not again be officially examined in the same depth as it had under the X-6 umbrella.

Rover and Friends

During the 1950s, nuclear propulsion was being explored for many applications, including aircraft and strategic ballistic missiles. At that time, no human had yet flown in space, but both the United States and the Soviet Union were working toward that end, and both sides envisioned a future in which outer space would be an extension of earthly battlefields.

As the United States Atomic Energy Commission undertook studies of nuclear propulsion for a wide range of vehicles during the 1950s, the most ambitious was the one that envisioned nuclear power for virtually unlimited human activities beyond earth orbit. Such work began in 1955 as a U.S. Air Force–sponsored weapons program at the Atomic Energy Commission's Los Alamos Scientific Laboratory in New Mexico. Designated as Project Rover, the idea was to develop a flight-rated nuclear rocket engine with seventy-five thousand pounds of thrust.

By 1958, Rover had evolved into an effort to develop a space-launch vehicle capable of taking people to Mars. The first experimental low-power test firing of a nuclear rocket engine, designated as Kiwi A, was in July 1959. (Rover is not to be confused with the parallel project code-named Orion that explored the use of a succession of nuclear explosions to create shock waves that would propel a vehicle through outer space. The obvious downside of such an approach would be that it would leave vast and infinitely expanding clouds of radioactive particles and debris in its wake.)

It was also in 1958 that Congress created the National Aeronautics and Space Administration (NASA) as the single federal agency that would serve as the umbrella for most American space activities. Among the programs that NASA inherited was Project Rover, which played into the NASA mandate for the development of large rockets for human space flight activities. Mainly, NASA concerned itself with vehicles powered by conventional rocket engines. The culmination of the NASA conventional efforts would be the massive Saturn launch vehicle that would ultimately take Apollo astronauts to the moon between 1969 and 1972. Standing 363 feet tall and powered by engines delivering 7.7 million pounds of thrust at launch, the Saturn V used in the Apollo lunar missions was the largest and most powerful rocket in history.

Saturn was heavily publicized throughout the 1960s, but few people knew that NASA was also working on nuclear propulsion, with an eye to eventually using this huge vehicle for a mission to Mars. This project from the early part of the decade was the nuclear engine for rocket vehicle application (NERVA) program that was managed by the newly created Space Nuclear Propulsion Office and was a direct successor to

It looks as though it might have been a 1950s drive-in under construction, but the Kiwi-A Prime was a nuclear reactor that underwent a highly successful full-power run on July 8, 1960, at Nevada Test Site in Jackass Flats, Nevada. Gaseous hydrogen was used as a propellant on the Kiwi-A tests that began in 1959. Kiwi-A served as a learning tool to test specifications and to discover changes that needed to be implemented in the next phase of study, the Kiwi-B series. *NASA*

A nuclear rocket engine being transported to its test stand. The first ground experimental nuclear rocket engine (XE) assembly (left) is shown here in cold-flow configuration, as it makes a late evening arrival at Engine Test Stand No. 1 at the Nuclear Rocket Development Station in Jackass Flats, Nevada. Cold-flow experiments are conducted using an assembly identical to the design used in power tests, except that the cold assembly does not contain any fissionable material or produce a nuclear reaction. Therefore, no fission power is generated. The large object at the right is one-half of an aluminum cylindrical closure that can be sealed around the engine, forming an airtight compartment, thereby permitting testing in a simulated space environment. *NASA*

The experimental engine cold flow (XECF) nuclear rocket engine assembly is shown being installed in Engine Test Stand No. 1 at the Nuclear Rocket Development Station in Jackass Flats, Nevada. In addition to the nozzle-reactor assembly, the XECF had two major subassemblies: an upper thrust module (attached to the test stand) and a lower thrust module, which contained propellant feed system components. This arrangement was used to facilitate remote removal and replacement of major subassemblies in the event of a malfunction. The cold-flow experimental engine underwent a series of tests designed to verify that the initial test stand was ready for hot engine testing, as well as to investigate engine startup under simulated altitude conditions and to check operating procedures not previously demonstrated. *NASA*

Project Rover. The actual hardware was built by Aerojet General Corporation.

The second Kiwi nuclear-engine test, designated as Kiwi A-Prime, was conducted at full power in July 1960, one year after Kiwi A, at the Nuclear Rocket Development Station at Jackass Flats, Nevada. The first in a series of Kiwi B tests was conducted in December 1961, followed by a series of reactor and engine experiments with such colorful code names as Phoebus, Peewee, and Nuclear Furnace.

Through 1971, the Space Nuclear Propulsion Office conducted nearly two dozen reactor and rocket engine tests, with some engines operating for as long as an hour and a half. These achieved thermal power output up to 4,500 megawatts and thrust up to two hundred

fifty thousand pounds. As this was going on, NASA officially unveiled its plan to send a six-man crew to the Martian surface. As described in official 1969 NASA documents, six astronauts would rendezvous with the NERVA-powered Mars vehicle in earth orbit and depart for Mars on November 12, 1981. They would arrive at Mars on August 9, 1982, and leave the NERVA ship in orbit while they descended to the Martian surface for a 10-week visit. The astronauts would then depart Mars on October 28, 1982, conduct a close flyby of Venus on February 28, 1983, and return to earth on August 14, 1983.

Shortly after Apollo 11 placed the first human on the moon in July 1969, the Nixon administration quietly cancelled the Mars mission. NERVA was officially, and quietly, terminated in 1973.

Timberwind

More than a decade after the cancellation of the NERVA program, the nuclear thermal propulsion concept for space flight resurfaced as Project Timberwind. Babcock & Wilcox built a subscale reactor for the Brookhaven National Laboratory in about 1985 under Project Pipe, and this seems to have been the basis for Timberwind, a "black" project not known outside the Strategic Defense Initiative Organization until April 1991.

It has subsequently been learned that the Timberwind program was initiated in November 1987 by Lieutenant General James Abrahamson, Director of the Strategic Defense Initiative Organization, and that it was managed by the air force's Phillips Laboratory at Kirtland Air Force Base in New Mexico.

The object of Timberwind was to develop a forty-megawatt particle-bed reactor (PBR) for space-launch activities. The earlier Project Pipe derived its name from the acronym for pulsed irradiation of PBR fuel element. Project Pipe had tested a subscale PBR model at the Sandia National Laboratory annular core research reactor (ACRR) located at Kirtland Air Force Base. These tests investigated the complex thermomechanical PBR fuel element system. Pipe 1, a test conducted in October 1988, achieved a peak output of 1,900 kilowatts. Pipe 2, in July 1989, experienced anomalies not seen earlier and was shut down less than half a minute into the experiment.

Timberwind would use nuclear thermal rockets (NTR), in which rocket fuel, such as hydrogen, flows through a reactor and is heated before flowing through the nozzle. Although the heat is no greater than that produced by a typical hydrogen/oxygen chemical rocket, there would be a higher specific impulse because hydrogen has a lower molecular weight than hydrogen plus oxygen.

In the fall of 1990, concepts were delivered to the Strategic Defense Initiative Organization outlining conversion of General Dynamics Atlas or Martin Marietta Titan launch vehicles to Timberwind test beds that would use eight NTRs, each with two hundred fifty thousand pounds of thrust. This could put up to seventy tons of payload into low-earth orbit.

Initially, Timberwind was to be the Strategic Defense Initiative Organization's means of launching large numbers of the Brilliant Pebbles interceptors discussed later in this volume. Eventually, other applications were also seriously considered. In July 1991, Stanley Browski at NASA's Nuclear Propulsion Systems Office told the International Conference on Emerging Nuclear Energy Systems, "If you want to initiate major lunar activity where significant amounts of cargo and people are sent to the moon routinely, nuclear thermal rockets can do it more efficiently and cost effectively than chemical rockets." This was, as the Strategic Defense Initiative Organization would have pointed out, certainly true of earth orbit, but Browski added the tantalizing promise of Timberwind NRVs doing what NERVA NRVs might have done a decade earlier—send humans on a fast trip to the planet Mars.

The Navy's Able "Charlie Victors"

Regardless of the potential of NTRs, Timberwind would not long survive the end of the Cold War. On October 18, 1991, the Department of Defense officially approved the termination of the Timberwind program. Apparently it was a slow death, though. On January 15, 1992, the Air Force Space Technology Test Center at Kirtland Air Force Base formally proposed using Timberwind as a system to make a six-month Mars mission a reality early in the twenty-first century.

Charlie Victor

When they were first theorized in 1716 by the great Swedish philosopher and inventor Emmanuel Swedenborg, air-cushion vehicles were probably categorized by most as rather curious gadgets. They were probably saying the same thing 150 years later, when the eccentric British inventor Sir John Thornycroft experimented with and patented working models of watercraft with air-lubricated hulls. By the second half of the twentieth century, however, such vessels had come into their own. People

This 1966 advertisement depicts an early Bell Aerospace Textron air cushion vehicle (ACV). Known to the U.S. Navy as Charlie Victor, it was the harbinger of the LCACs that would join the fleet a generation in the future.
Author's collection

dashed across the English Channel aboard hovercraft. In the United States, Bell Aerosystems, which became a division of Textron in 1960, was taking the lead in such vessels for the U.S. Navy.

In the 1960s, when the U.S. Navy evaluated its earliest air-cushion vehicles (ACV), they nicknamed the craft Charlie Victor (for the phonetic designations of C and V). The Defense Department specifically defines an ACV as a vehicle capable of being operated so that its weight, including its payload, is wholly or significantly supported on a continuously generated cushion, or bubble, of air at higher than ambient pressure.

After a further generation of Textron advanced-development craft were tested between 1977 and 1981, the navy authorized production of ACVs under the newly created ship class, landing craft air cushion (LCAC). The first El-Cacks joined the fleet in 1984, and by the end of the century, ninety-one had been delivered. Much larger than the Charlie Victors, they were eighty-one feet long off-cushion, and eighty-seven feet eleven inches long on-cushion, with a beam of forty-seven feet. Capable of carrying more than one hundred tons—including an M60 main battle tank—they had a speed of fifty knots.

Igloo White

In no weapons system ever conceived was the phrase "easier said than done" more appropriate. One of the strangest weapons systems ever conceived by the United States military coincidently involved the most sophisticated level of electronic computing power that had ever been deployed to a combat theater of operations. The era was that of the Vietnam War, and the curious project bore the tantalizingly cryptic code name Igloo White. Although it was publicly documented in the late 1970s, Igloo White contains may aspects that remained classified even into the twenty-first century. Today, it is largely forgotten.

The idea was fairly simple and straightforward, although the execution was extraordinarily complicated. The concept was to use miniaturized sound and vibration sensors to monitor foot and vehicle traffic on the Ho Chi Minh Trail, the network of infiltration routes that reached into southern and central South Vietnam from North Vietnam by way of Laos and Cambodia.

The Igloo White sensors themselves were air dropped onto the trail disguised as twigs and pieces of detritus that would blend into a mountainous jungle environment. However, these sensors were so sophisticated that they could detect not only the noise and the vibration of passing vehicles, but things as subtle as body heat. The Doppler effect of multiple sensors could also determine the direction that a vehicle or person was moving. This data could theoretically be relayed to attack aircraft, which could then attack the site without seeing the target visually.

When it was first presented to him in the autumn of 1966, the scheme found an energetic champion in the person of Secretary of Defense Robert Strange McNamara. Being enthralled with the potential of any emerging advanced technology, McNamara ordered that the project be implemented and given a high priority. As it was being developed, the project was known variously as air launched acoustical reconnaissance (ALARS) or trails and roads interdiction, multi-sensor (TRIM). The sensors themselves

Heading out on an Igloo White mission, a U.S. Air Force EC-121R Batcat of the 553rd Reconnaissance Wing taxis onto the runway at Korat Royal Thai Air Force Base in January 1969. The Batcats flew dozen-hour missions relaying sensor data from the Ho Chi Minh Trail to Nakhon Phanom, home to what was then the largest computer complex in the Far East.
U.S. Air Force

were based on the air-dropped sounding buoys (sonobouys, which are used in oceans) that were then used by the U.S. Navy to track Soviet submarines. The first sensors were acoustic buoys, referred to as acoubuoys, which are used exclusively on land. Sonobouys recorded the acoustic signatures of the sounds of the engines and propellers of various Soviet submarine types. The recordings were kept in libraries and used to identify and track Soviet vessels and monitor Soviet technology. The idea was to apply the same process to land operations.

In fact, the acoubuoys were only one of the types of sensors that were included in the Igloo White project. While the acoubuoys detected sound, other sensors detected vibration and others monitored temperature anomalies. Some sensors were tiny, while others were several inches square and weighed several pounds. They were very sophisticated for the time, given the fact that they had to be designed to distinguish between the sound and/or vibration of a user of the trail and phenomena such as distant thunder or artillery fire. Tens of thousands of the sensing devices would be manufactured and sent overseas though 1972.

Deployment of the secret sensors was undertaken initially by the secret U.S. Navy observation squadron VO-67 (OBSRON 67) that operated Lockheed P-2 Neptunes under code name Sophomore between November 1967 and June 1968. Seven Neptunes were also operated by the U.S. Air Force under the designation B-69. In 1967 and early 1968, the navy operated the program under such operational code names as Dye Marker and Muscle Shoals. It was not until the U.S. Air Force took over the management of the project in June 1968 that the Igloo White code name was assigned. The Air Force 21st Special Operations Squadron used H-3 helicopters to sow the sensors, although fixed-wing aircraft continued to be utilized as well. South Vietnamese troops also placed many of the sensors by hand.

Though the sensors were small and unobtrusive, everything else about Igloo White was massive. First, there was its budget. Igloo White was funded to the tune of a billion dollars annually (more than five times that in today's dollars). Between 1967 and 1972, the operations center occupied the largest building in Southeast Asia,

a place known as the Infiltration Surveillance Center (ISC), that was located at the Royal Thai air base at Nakhon Phanom (aka Naked Phantom). Inside the ISC was the largest computer and data processing center in Southeast Asia.

Operationally, the sensors could transmit only about twenty miles, so the data had to be relayed to the ISC by aircraft flying over the Ho Chi Minh Trail. From 1968 through 1971, the air force data-relay missions were flown by the EC-121R Batcats of the 553rd Reconnaissance Wing, based at Korat RTAFB in Thailand. Each was equipped with eight ARR-52 data receivers for listening to the sensors hidden below. Typical Batcat missions involved as much as twelve hours or more of flight time, most of it spent overflying the Ho Chi Minh Trail recording and transmitting data from the sensors. In order to ensure seamless coverage, each EC-121R would remain on station over the trail until the next one arrived from Korat to take over. Beginning in 1970, the Batcats were replaced by the smaller Beechcraft QU-22 Quackers in the Igloo White operations and assigned to the 554th Reconnaissance Wing at Udorn Royal Thai Air Force Base.

Inside the huge climate-controlled ISC, a staff numbering in the hundreds worked with numerous IBM 360 and IBM 2400 mainframe computers to evaluate the data. The total computing power at the ISC was virtually unmatched at that time anywhere in the world. The IBM 2250 monitors displayed detailed views of the Ho Chi Minh trail on which individual sensors tracked individual infiltrators who could not imagine the technology that kept track of them. So capable were the big IBMs that they could tell how fast vehicles were traveling and the weight of their loads.

When the data was processed, it went out to attack aircraft—including AC-47, AC-119, or AC-130 gunships or F-4 fighter bombers—that could strike quickly before the enemy eluded them. This worked well in theory, but often times, even though the staff at the ISC could "see" an enemy, the process of getting bombs on the target was delayed by the necessity of sending a request for targeting authority through the chain of command. The usefulness of Igloo White was further compromised by a clever enemy who learned how to distort the data being streamed back to the ISC. The enemy was also using bicycles and people walking to transport materiel on the Ho Chi Minh Trail. While bikes were detectable, it was virtually impossible for attack aircraft to hit them.

Spy Satellites

Few systems from the second decade of the Cold War better embody the notion of supersecret high-tech gadgetry than spy satellites. By the late 1950s, both sides were working on them with great urgency, and by the mid 1960s, both sides had them in service, keeping tabs on one another's ICBM development programs. Such spacecraft were known to exist, but the details of even the earliest and most rudimentary were unknown outside rarified clandestine circles until practically the end of the twentieth century.

In the United States, the technological history of reconnaissance and surveillance satellites is known to have begun in 1953 with a supersecret U.S. Air Force program known simply as Weapons System (WS) 117L. It was actually not one, but at least three systems. These included Sentry (later known as satellite and missile observation system, or SAMOS) and the missile detection alarm system (MIDAS), as well as the best known, the photo-reconnaissance satellite family known as Corona. MIDAS used an infrared sensor to detect the flash from a missile being launched. SAMOS, which remained top

secret past the turn of the century, is known to have had an early generation that used a recoverable film capsule system like Corona. A second-generation SAMOS used a radio-relay system to return digital imagery.

Corona

In March 1956, Lockheed Space Systems was awarded the contract to build the first of a series of reconnaissance spacecraft. The program was known as Corona, and the actual spacecraft would be code-named Keyhole and carry designations with the prefix KH. This was a year before the world's first satellite had orbited. When that satellite turned out to be the Soviet Sputnik 1, the urgency of Keyhole was clearly underscored. Of course, when the Soviets shot down the U-2 flown by Francis Gary Powers in 1960, it was clear that manned reconnaissance overflights were no longer feasible, and Corona and Keyhole went from highly desirable to vitally essential.

In the wake of Sputnik, the United States Department of Defense ordered that WS-117L be expedited. Because of the number of people

Since 1960, the National Reconnaissance Office (NRO) has overseen development and deployment of United States reconnaissance satellites. A Defense Department agency, it is staffed by Defense and CIA personnel. NRO

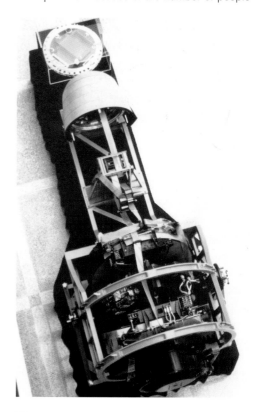

This is a close-up view of a Corona reconnaissance satellite on display at the Central Intelligence Agency headquarters. *Courtesy Center for the Study of National Reconnaissance*

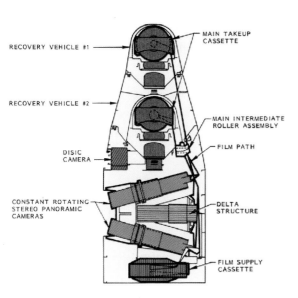

RECOVERY VEHICLE #1
MAIN TAKEUP CASSETTE
RECOVERY VEHICLE #2
MAIN INTERMEDIATE ROLLER ASSEMBLY
DISIC CAMERA
FILM PATH
CONSTANT ROTATING STEREO PANORAMIC CAMERAS
DELTA STRUCTURE
FILM SUPPLY CASSETTE

A detailed cross section shows the inner components of the Corona J-3 reconnaissance satellite. *Courtesy Center for the Study of National Reconnaissance*

Transports

Bombers

This photograph was taken by a Corona reconnaissance satellite in August 1966. It compares heavy bombers and selected transport aircraft at Dolon Air Field in the Soviet Union. *Courtesy Center for the Study of National Reconnaissance*

who would necessarily have to be involved in such a complex project, it was decided that a cover story would be developed. The air force would announce a "scientific satellite" program called Discoverer. This name would serve as Corona's cover for the first thirty-eight missions.

The operational hardware within the Corona Keyholes included Itek panoramic cameras containing sixteen thousand feet of Eastman Kodak 70mm strip film. This film stock offered resolution down to thirty-five feet during missions in the 1950s, and five feet by 1967. The first Corona satellites weighed 1,650 pounds, including their cameras and their 80 pounds of Kodak film. The last of the Corona-series Keyholes, the KH-4Bs, weighed 6,600 pounds. They were all launched from Vandenberg Air Force Base in California by the U.S. Air Force using a Thor launch vehicle topped with an Agena upper stage.

As with photo-reconnaissance aircraft, Corona would take pictures using negative film that would be processed and printed. Satellites would drop film canisters into the atmosphere, where they would be snatched in midair by specially configured transport aircraft operated by the U.S. Air Force's 6593rd Test Squadron, which was based at Hickam Air Force Base in Hawaii, located across the runway from Honolulu International Airport. Initially, this squadron used Fairchild C-119Js, but in 1962, they switched to

Lockheed JC-130Bs. The C-119Js could handle the smaller 200-pound capsules, but the JC-130Bs could recover the capsules used in the later Corona missions that weighed as much as three thousand pounds.

The first successful test launch, designated as Discoverer 1, occurred on February 28, 1959. Discoverer 2, launched in April, was the first to carry a film capsule, but the capsule was ejected at the wrong place and lost. Problems with the Corona system, mainly due to the Thor missile rather than the Keyhole spacecraft, very nearly resulted in the program being cancelled before it really got started. The thirteenth mission, on August 10, 1960, proved to be lucky thirteen. Though the KH-1 spacecraft was carrying just a dummy film capsule, everything worked perfectly. The timing was good.

After Francis Gary Powers and his U-2 spy plane were shot down on May 1, 1960, manned

Technicians are seen handling a Corona satellite film-return capsule. *Courtesy Center for the Study of National Reconnaissance*

basic KH-4 was used on twenty successful missions between February 1962 and December 1963, exposing more than 239,000 feet of film. This period of service coincided with the Cuban Missile Crisis of October 1962 and its aftermath. The mission in February 1962, announced as Discoverer 38, was the first Corona mission to provide stereoscopic imagery. The first Keyholes to carry two film capsules, the KH-4As, were used in forty-nine successful missions, exposing 1.3 million feet of film between August 1963 and October 1969. The KH-4B spacecraft were in service between September 1967 and May 1972, averaging 32,000 feet of film over sixteen successful missions.

The first thirty-eight Corona launches were "covered" with Discoverer designations. Beginning in 1962, the Corona launches were kept secret and no longer given Discoverer numbers.

After the KH-4 series, the Corona project concluded, and new code names were assigned to missions flown by subsequent Keyhole types. Under the Argon program, the 2,800-pound KH-5 flew seven successful missions through August 1964. The 3,300-pound KH-6 used in the short-lived Lanyard program used a pair of sixty-six-inch-focal-length panoramic cameras to create stereoscopic three-dimensional images.

Later film-return Keyhole spacecraft operated under the Gambit program. Gambit began in the mid-1960s, while Corona was still ongoing, and continued into the 1980s, when film-return technology was superseded by the digital imaging of the huge KH-11 spacecraft. Still secret a decade past the end of the Cold War, the satellites of Project Gambit carried cameras with a resolution of eighteen inches for early KH-7s and six inches for the close-look KH-8. The KH-7s weighed about 4,500 pounds and had an operational life of about a week. The KH-8 Gambits weighed 3.3 tons and were designed to have a life of two months in which to return film in two independent film capsules. The first KH-7 mission was flown in July 1963, and the KH-8 satellite made its debut in July 1966. The KH-8s would typically be launched in the early spring and operate through the summer. Operationally, they complemented the larger, higher-flying KH-9s, which would go up a few weeks later and operate through the end of the year. The last KH-8 mission is believed to have been launched in April 1984.

reconnaissance flights over the Soviet Union had been terminated, so Corona arrived just in time. On August 18, Discoverer 14 successfully returned a capsule containing film. The sixteen thousand feet of film contained clear images with higher-than-expected resolution that amazed and delighted the CIA analysts.

The second-generation KH-2 series made its debut in October 1960, and was succeeded by the similar KH-3 series, which flew five successful missions between August 1961 and January 1962. By the end of 1961, the Corona program had quietly confirmed that the Soviet Union had deployed only about two dozen ICBMs—rather than the nearly two hundred that were a subject of concern during the 1960 presidential election campaign.

Whereas the first three Keyhole satellite types were fitted with a single camera, the KH-4 series had two: one looking forward, the other aft. The

In service for nearly two decades, the KH-8s were the longest-serving class of film-return photo-reconnaissance satellites used by the United States. They were retired because of the decision to switch from film to high-resolution digital photography.

The KH-9 of Project Hexagon came on line while Project Gambit was still operational, and the two operated concurrently and probably cooperatively for more than a decade. Best known by the nickname Big Bird, the KH-9 satellites of Project Hexagon were more than twice the size of the earlier Keyhole satellites. They each weighed 12.5 tons and were launched by the Titan 3C heavy-lift launch vehicle. Whereas earlier Keyholes carried one or two film capsules, the Big Birds had four. Whereas the life of earlier Keyholes was measured in days or weeks, the KH-9s were designed to serve for nine months or more. This allowed more than one to be on station at all times to provide continuous photo-reconnaissance coverage of areas of interest within the Soviet Union and elsewhere. Like the Gambit Keyholes, the Hexagon Big Birds carried cameras with a ground resolution measured in inches, and some carried large mapping cameras. The first of about twenty Hexagon launches came in June 1971, and the last was on April 18, 1986, the 211th anniversary of the first United States early-warning mission, the famous midnight ride of Paul Revere.

All of the Keyholes except Project Dorian, the Douglas KH-10 manned orbiting laboratory, were built by Lockheed Space Systems. Initially, all were assembled at Menlo Park, near San Francisco, California, but in the 1960s, the whole operation was moved to a new Lockheed facility at nearby Sunnyvale. The remarkable Hubble Space Telescope, which was built by Lockheed at Sunnyvale for NASA in the mid-1980s and launched in 1990, is thought to be similar to, and a sister ship of, the later Keyhole satellites.

Though both MIDAS and SAMOS remain veiled in secrecy, Corona's activities through 1972 were officially declassified by President Bill Clinton in a February 1995 executive order. It was not until Corona came in from the cold in 1995 that we began to understand how truly vast and far-reaching the United States satellite intelligence program had been.

Technicians install the protective fairing over a MIDAS 6 Series III satellite payload, which sits atop an Agena B prior to launch from Vandenberg Air Force Base in November 1962. *Courtesy Center for the Study of National Reconnaissance*

Vela

A U.S. Air Force program with the Spanish name Vela (which means vigilance and suggests the notion of a guardian) was the first United States nuclear explosion detection system. Originally code-named Vela Hotel, the project began in 1960 with input from NASA, the Atomic Energy Commission, the Defense Advanced Research Projects Agency (DARPA), and the Air Force's Ballistic Missile Division, and it was part of a broader nuclear detection system. The sensors for the Vela satellite would be built by the AEC's Sandia and Los Alamos Laboratories in New Mexico, while the satellite itself would be built by the Thompson Ramo Woolridge Company (TRW) in Southern California. The Velas were essentially a pair of twenty-six-sided polyhedrons with sensors on most faces. The satellites stood four feet seven inches tall and weighed between three hundred and five hundred pounds.

While the Keyholes and MIDAS operated in relatively low orbit, the *Vela* satellites were in orbit generally between sixty thousand and seventy thousand miles above the earth's surface. The *Vela* spacecraft were launched in pairs using two separate boosters, with the first two sent aloft in October 1963 in time to monitor the 1963 Nuclear Test Ban Treaty. Subsequent *Vela* dual launches occurred in July 1964 and July 1965. An advanced *Vela* development program

Launched in pairs, as shown in this photograph, the U.S. Air Force Vela nuclear detection spacecraft were multi-sided polyhedrons. The first two were launched on October 17, 1963, and launches continued into the 1980s. Each Vela was designed to have a service life of about six months. *U.S. Air Force*

superseded the original *Vela* series in 1965, and these were first launched in April 1967. Again, it was a pair of satellites launched together on the same day using a pair of Titan 3C boosters. Additional dual launches occurred May 1969 and April 1970.

Composed of a pair of polyhedrons, the peanut-shaped advanced *Velas* weighed seven hundred pounds and stood five feet tall on the factory floor. The newer craft were capable of detecting both subterranean and atmospheric nuclear explosions. They also took on the secondary task of monitoring solar radiation in conjunction with United States manned Apollo space missions.

In contrast to the disappointing MIDAS program, *Vela* worked extremely well. The original *Velas* operated for more than five years, and the later models all had useful lives of more than a decade. Indeed, they were all still functioning in 1984 when the *Vela* system was deliberately powered down and its mission assumed by the Defense Support Program.

White Cloud

The White Cloud spacecraft were a series of secret ocean-surveillance satellites used by the U.S. Navy to monitor the movement of Soviet

ships and submarines. Developed for the Naval Research Laboratory by Martin Marietta, they were part of the naval ocean surveillance system (NOSS), which monitored radio traffic and radar transmissions using triangulation.

First launched in April 1976, the White Cloud satellites operated in orbits 700 miles above the earth. As with MIDAS satellites, White Clouds carried small hitchhiker satellites that were deployed after reaching orbit. The White Clouds and their hitchhikers operated in clouds, or clusters. The last two are believed to have been launched in February 1986 and May 1987.

The White Cloud project was so secret that Naval Research Laboratory personnel were not even permitted to use the phrase in telephone conversations—that is, until souvenir postal covers with pictures of a White Cloud satellite and Vandenberg Air Force Base postage cancellations showed up for sale at the tourist gift shop in the cafeteria at NASA's Johnson Space Center in October 1984!

This illustration of the supersecret White Cloud ocean-surveillance U.S. Navy spacecraft was done by the author for his best-selling 1985 book, *The Encyclopedia of U.S. Spacecraft*. At that time, the White Cloud configuration had just been revealed on a souvenir postal cover at the tourist gift shop in the cafeteria at NASA's Johnson Space Center. *Author's illustration*

Killing Spy Satellites

As noted above, Weapons System (WS) 117L was a family of U.S. Air Force spy satellites. In turn, there would be WS-199, a family of anti-satellite weapons. In 1957, the Strategic Air Command undertook this supersecret project, which evolved into three specific air-launched anti-satellite weapons. These would be designated with series letter suffixes to WS-199. All were based on the Sperry MGM-29 Sergeant, a U.S. Army artillery missile. The weapons were test fired from a B-47 Stratojet strategic bomber, but the intended launch platform would have been the B-58 Hustler supersonic bomber.

The thirty-seven-foot-long Martin WS-199B Bold Orion was test fired a dozen times in 1958 and 1959. In the last such firing, in June 1959, the Bold Orion targeted the orbiting Explorer 4 satellite, coming within 4 miles of it at an altitude of 156 miles.

The thirty-foot-long Lockheed WS-199C High Virgo was test fired four times through September 1959, achieving speeds up to Mach 6. These flights included another attempted near miss of Explorer 4, but failed to come anywhere close to the satellite. The cause was found to be a failed communications link, and the High Virgo weapon was then grounded. The forty-six-foot-long McDonnell WS-199D Alpha Draco was the subject of three tests in 1959, but little more is known. Though its full parameters remain cloaked in secrecy even today, the Weapons System 199 program appears to have been terminated at the end of 1959 without an operational system having been deployed.

Squanto Terror

With its particularly fearsome code name, Squanto Terror was the test component of Air Force Program 437, which was the first practical anti-satellite weapon deployed operationally by the United States. The system involved a Thor-launched spacecraft carrying a nuclear weapon that could knock out Soviet spacecraft by electromagnetic pulse.

The fear was not so much of spy satellites, but of orbiting weapons. Soviet Premier Nikita Khrushchev had threatened to orbit nuclear weapons under a program that is now known to have been the R-36-O fractional orbital bombardment system. In response, AFP-437 was initiated and given the highest priority among air force development projects.

AFP-437 was loosely based on technology developed between 1958 and 1962 by the U.S. Air Force's Air Research and Development Command, the Defense Advanced Research Projects Agency, and other agencies during numerous studies of both anti-satellite weapons and defenses against them. It was developed by the Air Force Ballistic Missile Division with the improbable acronym SAINT (for SAtellite INspecTor). Though it was cancelled in December 1962, the technical ground that it covered made SAINT the grandfather of even today's United States anti-satellite systems.

Between 1958 and 1962, the Department of Defense had conducted nuclear anti-satellite tests under Project Argus and Project Fishbowl. The Fishbowl detonation in July 1962 (code-named Starfish) had literally fried the electronics

Still a mystery after all of these years, the forty-six-foot McDonnell WS-199D Alpha Draco was designed to destroy Soviet nuclear weapons in space. Alpha Dracos were test fired three times during 1959, demonstrating lifting-body flight not previously possible at Mach 5 within the atmosphere. *Author's collection*

The Project Dorian KH-10 manned orbiting laboratory would have been thirty feet eight inches long, with a diameter of ten feet. It would have weighed nineteen-thousand pounds at launch and would have had a habitable volume of four-hundred cubic feet. That would have been enough room for two astronauts to work in a shirt-sleeves environment. Each two-man crew would have served a thirty-day tour of duty aboard an MOL, and then would have been replaced by another crew on a thirty-day rotation. Crews would commute to and from the MOLs in Blue Gemini spacecraft based on NASA's Geminis. *McDonnell Douglas*

Inside the MOL mockup. The space station was designed to enclose a shirt-sleeves environment, but a space suit would have been used when passing to and from the Gemini capsule. *McDonnell Douglas*

of several observer satellites with high-energy particles that were driven at high speed by a nuclear explosion, which occurred at an altitude of 250 miles. This was the catalyst for the idea of an anti-satellite weapon that used radiation, rather than a direct hit.

Beginning in February 1964, the Squanto Terror test firings involved anti-satellite weapons launched by Thor boosters from Johnson Island in the Pacific to intercept missiles launched from Vandenberg Air Force Base in California. The first tests went so well that the third interception, in April 1964, was conducted by personnel of the Air (later Aerospace) Defense Command's 10th Aerospace

Defense Squadron, the same people who would have used the anti-satellite weapons operationally. Squanto Terror became an operational system in June 1964.

Two nuclear anti-satellite weapons went on alert at Johnson Island, ready for an actual launch against live Soviet targets. The reason that this location in the South Pacific was chosen was that the fractional orbital bombardment system would have involved ICBMs launched from the Soviet Union that would travel across the South Pole and approach the United States from the south.

Project Dorian

In the days before NASA solidified its control over America's manned space program, the U.S. Air Force imagined itself to have a manifest destiny of not only putting humans in space, but also of establishing a continuous presence in space. It was not until the 1990s that NASA established a permanent place for itself in earth orbit, and that was by way of its astronauts serving as guests aboard the Russian (former Soviet) Mir space station, and later aboard the International Space Station. Had the U.S. Air Force had its way, the service would have had a continuous manned presence in space a generation earlier.

The initial studies for a semi-permanent manned air force base in outer space dated back to 1959, a year after NASA had been created to spearhead America's first effort to put astronauts into space. The air force saw NASA as having the job of pioneering space exploration, but imagined itself as having a mandate to establish an operational presence in earth orbit. Under the secret code name Project Dorian, the manned orbiting laboratory (MOL) program envisioned a galaxy of relatively inexpensive manned space stations that could be used on an almost continuous basis.

The tactical reason for MOL was reconnaissance. The air force sought an alternative to using manned reconnaissance aircraft to overfly the Soviet Union—especially after one of their U-2s was shot down on May 1, 1960, in a massively embarrassing international incident. MOL represented a much-needed improvement over U-2 technology. Instead of braving thousands of miles of hostile airspace and uncertain weather, the MOL astronauts would float high above the range of Soviet countermeasures, snapping the shutters of their Hasselblads for weeks at a time.

Congress authorized $1.5 billion in August 1965, and formal contracts were issued. The MOL space station would be built by the Douglas Aircraft Company's Missile and Space Systems Division (MSSD) Space Systems Center in Huntington Beach, California. In 1967, when Douglas merged with the McDonnell Aircraft Corporation, makers of the Mercury and Gemini, MSSD would become the McDonnell Douglas Astronautics Company. The launch vehicle for MOL would be the Martin Titan 3C, a variation on the Titan 2 that served as the launch vehicle for the NASA Gemini spacecraft and as an ICBM.

The MOL was to be officially designated as KH-10, placing it in the same numbering sequence as the Keyhole family of unmanned photo-reconnaissance satellites that had been in development since the 1950s. The KH-10 was the only Keyhole not to be designed by Lockheed, and the only one that was to have carried a human crew.

The MOL crews would have staffed the KH-10s on a thirty-day rotation, commuting to and from their duty stations in Blue Gemini spacecraft based on NASA's Geminis. Each crew would have included a photographer as well as a photo-interpreter, who had a laboratory in which to process the film. With an interpreter aboard, it could be known rather quickly if another photo of something was needed, and ninety minutes later, the mission would be over the same place on the earth and the photographer could take another picture. This was seen as a clear improvement over existing aerial or satellite reconnaissance that involved getting the film to the ground for processing and interpretation.

Initially, it was imagined that the first MOL would be built and deployed into earth orbit by the end of 1968, but in 1967 the schedule slipped, first to 1970, and later to 1972. By early 1968, the MOL mockup was completed, static structural tests of flight-representative assemblies were under way, and air force crews were undergoing training using surplus NASA Gemini capsules. By the spring of 1969, there were several MOLs under construction in Building 45 at the McDonnell Douglas Space Systems Center in Huntington Beach, California. Suddenly, on June 10, a month before NASA's historic Apollo 11 lunar landing, the MOL project was terminated by the Nixon administration. The reasons for the cancellation ranged from cost (the usual bugaboo) to a turf war between the Department of Defense and the CIA over who was going to manage space-based intelligence assets, and between the U.S. Air Force and NASA over who was going to manage space stations.

The MOLs were taken out of Building 45 under heavy guard and presumably destroyed. All of the MOL astronauts were transferred to NASA, where they would eventually find themselves in the space shuttle program. One of them, Richard Truly, made two space shuttle flights and went on to serve as NASA's administrator from 1986 to 1992. The air force and the Department of Defense never had another space station program. NASA confidently predicted a one-hundred-man space station by the end of the 1970s, but the only space station that was ever owned and operated by NASA was the three-man Skylab that was inhabited briefly in 1973 and 1974.

Attempts by NASA to field a space station in the 1980s and early 1990s never came to fruition, but the agency became a major participant in the international space station that was first staffed by a crew in 1999. The Soviet Union, meanwhile, went on to develop a series of successful space stations. These were based, ironically, on information that they had gleaned from spying on Project Dorian.

The manned orbiting laboratory is seen here under construction at the McDonnell Douglas facility in Huntington Beach, California, circa 1969. *McDonnell Douglas*

Sea Whiz

One of the most remarkable, if little heralded, weapons systems developed and deployed by the U.S. Navy during the last half of the Cold War was the 20mm Phalanx Mk.15 close-in weapons system (CIWS), with the acronym pronounced as "Sea Whiz." The Phalanx is a six-barreled Gatling gun that is designed to engage, track, and kill enemy cruise missiles or aircraft that might threaten U.S. Navy vessels at sea. It is described as a terminal defense system, meaning that it is deployed against close-range targets that may have penetrated outer fleet defenses. Though it was originally deployed at the end of the 1970s, the Sea Whiz remains the principal naval terminal air defense system today.

The original Sea Whizzes had a rate of fire of 3,000 rounds per minute, but by the 1990s, newer Phalanxes could fire 4,500 rounds per minute. The rounds were originally made of heavy armor-piercing depleted uranium, but later tungsten rounds were found to be easier to store and handle. Of the Sea Whiz's targets, it is said that, "If it flies, it dies."

Created by General Dynamics' Pomona Division (later Hughes Missile Systems), the Phalanx was first tested at sea aboard the USS *Bigelow* (DD-942) in 1977. The Sea Whiz was an immediate success, and the navy was soon retrofitting its entire fleet of combat and amphibious warfare ships with them. Each Phalanx weapons system

A Phalanx Sea Whiz stands guard as the USS *New Jersey* steams out of port in San Francisco in August 1985. Note the World War II–vintage five-inch gun turret in the foreground. *Bill Yenne*

consists of a pair of 20mm gun mounts, plus the VPS-2 pulse-Doppler fire-control system that contains a search radar for threat detection and a tracking radar for aiming the gun. The distinctive closed-loop fire control tracks both the incoming target and the stream of outgoing projectiles, allowing the Sea Whiz to adjust its aim to hit fast-moving targets.

The later Block 1B Phalanx surface mode (PSUM) system contains side-mounted forward-looking infrared (FLIR) radar and a thermal imager automatic acquisition video tracker (AAVT), thus permitting the weapon to engage low, slow, or hovering helicopters, as well as surface craft. The USS *Cole* (DDG-67), damaged in an al Qaeda surface attack in Yemen in 2000, was not equipped with a Block 1B Sea Whiz at the time, although it has since been retrofitted. This weapon could have defeated this strike, and the U.S. Navy and its Sea Whiz gunners have since been on guard for an attempted repeat of the attack.

This is one of the Phalanx Sea Whiz guns aboard the USS *New Jersey* (BB-62), as photographed by the author in August 1985. Note the three kill markings that chronicle successful tests of this particular weapon. *Bill Yenne*

Midgetman's Big Rig

In the late 1980s, drivers on the highways through the wide-open spaces of Montana's Chouteau and Cascade counties occasionally saw a strange, enormous tractor-trailer. Perhaps the largest and most interesting wheeled land vehicle ever operated exclusively by the U.S. Air Force was the hardened mobile launcher truck. It was developed for use by the MGM-134 small ICBM (SICBM), which was known as the Midgetman because it was smaller than existing ICBMs.

During the military buildup of the 1980s, numerous proposals were made and pursued in an effort to select a successor to the U.S. Air Force's thousand-missile inventory of silo-based Boeing LGM-30 Minuteman ICBMs. The multiple-warhead, silo-based Martin Marietta LGM-118 Peacekeeper was ultimately chosen, but only to augment, not replace, the Minuteman. Meanwhile, there were numerous proposals for basing modes other than traditional underground silos. Against this backdrop, the Martin Marietta MGM-134 was also considered to augment the Minuteman in order to give the U.S. Air Force a mobile basing mode for increased survivability. As had been the case with both the Minuteman and Peacekeeper, trains had been considered and rejected as a basing mode, so it was decided to put the Midgetmen on trucks. President Reagan authorized full-scale development of the system in December 1986.

Enter the hardened mobile launcher. The idea was that in time of war or national emergency, dozens of them would take to the road and scatter across the sparsely populated northern plains and drive randomly until ordered to stop and launch.

Boeing Aerospace was the prime contractor for the project, and the actual truck itself was built by Seattle-based PACCAR (formerly Pacific Car and Foundry), the umbrella holding company of America's leading manufacturers of Class 8 trucks, Kenworth and Peterbilt. Also involved in the system were Loral Defense Systems Division and Goodyear, who made the big tires, fourteen of which were used on each vehicle. Delivered to Malmstrom Air Force Base at Great Falls, Montana, for testing, the tractor-launcher combination weighed 119.5 tons and had a drawbar pull capability of more than 40 tons. The engines by Allison and Cummins Diesel drove eight tractor wheels through an electro-hydraulic transmission.

The big rig was listed as having a top highway speed of fifty-five miles per hour—because the United States was still operating under the draconian national speed limit—but it also had off-road capabilities. For launch, there was a trailer-mounted plow to dig the launcher into the ground. As described in an advertisement from 1986, during the test, the vehicle "shouldered its way through a field strewn with fourteen-inch boulders, clawed across gullies and up ravine walls, plowed through sand at speeds that would earn a ticket on most city streets, then waltzed through a slalom built in one of the world's worst mud puddles."

The hardened mobile launcher continued its field tests until 1991, around the time that the Midgetman missile made its first successful flight test. This launch, on April 18, 1991, was not from

Seen here dashing through the snow of the Montana winter, circa 1987, is the big rig that served as the hardened mobile launcher for the Midgetman SICBM. It was built by the makers of Kenworth and Peterbilt trucks, familiar names on the nation's highways.
Author's collection

Tank crews operate with multiple integrated laser engagement system (MILES) hardware at the National Training Center at Fort Irwin, California, circa 1990. Each individual and vehicle in the exercise has a detection system to sense hits and perform casualty assessments. Laser transmitters can be seen attached to the helmets of the soldiers. *Loral*

the truck in Montana, but from a silo at Vandenberg Air Force Base in California. By the end of the year, the Cold War was over, and President George Herbert Walker Bush canceled the Midgetman program in January 1992.

MILES

Developed by the U.S. Army Program Executive Office for Simulation, Training, and Instrumentation (PEO STRI), the multiple integrated laser engagement system (MILES) was initiated to provide tactical engagement simulation for direct-fire force-on-force training using eye-safe laser "bullets." It's like paintball with focused light—and far cleaner than with paint.

As described by PEO STRI, within MILES each individual and vehicle in the training exercise has a detection system to sense hits and perform casualty assessment. Laser transmitters are attached to each individual's and vehicle's weapon system and accurately replicate actual ranges and lethality of the specific weapon systems.

During the latter years of the twentieth century, MILES training was reportedly shown to dramatically increase the combat readiness and fighting effectiveness of military forces. In addition to providing an integrated training system for direct-fire force-on-force training, MILES significantly reduced life-cycle costs of hardware, while using new technology to increase accuracy and flexibility. Within MILES, the main gun simulation system (MGSS) and the direct-indirect fire cueing system would be key elements in the combat training center instrumentation systems used to simulate battlefield effect.

On the individual level, MILES dramatically reduced the size and weight of the system to make it easier for the soldiers using it to forget that they have a system monitoring what they are doing. MILES also included an after-action review capability.

Dragon MAW

Shoulder-fired like the World War II bazooka and the later SMAW and Javelin, the M47 Dragon medium anti-armor weapon (MAW) was a wire-guided antitank guided missile first deployed with the U.S. Army, Europe (USAREUR), in January 1975. Produced by McDonnell Douglas, it was designed to kill tanks and destroy fortified enemy positions. The Dragon's missile was guided, but unlike later fire-and-forget weapons, the gunner had to keep the target aligned in the sights until impact. This duration was calculated at 11.2 seconds for a target at a range of one thousand meters (3,281 feet). The M47 weighed in at 33.9 pounds with the day-tracker sight or 48.7 pounds with the thermal night-tracker sight.

In 1985, the U.S. Marine Corps initiated a product improvement program (PIP) managed by the Naval Surface Warfare Center (NSWC) Dahlgren Division, that led to the Dragon II, with an increase in range to 1,500 meters and a substantial improvement in warhead penetration. By the 1990s, the U.S. Army had acquired 7,000 of the weapons, and the marines had 1,978 in their inventory. The technology evolved into the Javelin shoulder-launched weapon that is fielded today.

SMAW

First fielded in 1984, the shoulder-launched multi-purpose assault weapon (SMAW) was designed

The M47 Dragon was considered light enough to be carried and fired by a single infantryman. It weighed nearly fifty pounds with its Night Tracker, so the infantryman wouldn't have wanted to carry both the Dragon *and* his full battle gear. *McDonnell Douglas*

as a portable anti-armor rocket launcher. At that time, the SMAW included the Mk.153 launcher, the Mk.3 high-explosive dual-purpose (HEDP) encased rocket, the Mk.4 practice rocket, and the Mk.217 9-mm spotting cartridge. The Mk.6 encased high-explosive anti-armor (HEAA) rocket was added to the inventory a decade later. SMAW was originally a bunker-buster design tested to penetrate up to eighteen feet of sandbags. The antitank capability was added during Operation Desert Storm. The SMAW was 54 inches long when ready to fire, but folded down to 29.9 inches for carrying. It weighed 16.6 pounds empty, 29.5 pounds with an HEDP round, and 30.5 pounds with an HEAA round.

The SMAW Mk.153 launcher was based on the Israeli B-300 and consisted of the launch tube, the spotting rifle, the firing mechanism, and mounting brackets. The launch tube is fiberglass/epoxy with a gel coat on the bore. The early SMAW demonstrated several shortcomings, and a series of modifications addressed the deficiencies in the 1990s. These included a resleeving process for bubbled launch tubes, a kit that reduced environmental intrusion into the trigger mechanism, and an optical sight modification to allow the new HEAA rocket to be used effectively against moving armored targets.

Though SMAW was introduced as a Marine Corps–unique system, 150 launchers and 5,000 rockets were provided to the U.S. Army during Desert Storm. At the end of 1995, there were 1,364 SMAWs in the United States inventory.

Copperhead

Introduced in the late 1970s, the U.S. Army's Martin Marietta M712 Copperhead was a revolutionary weapon that was very ahead of its time. It was the first-ever smart artillery projectile. It looked like a missile, but had no propulsion. Therefore, it is properly categorized as a projectile. Its smarts derived from its having an internal guidance system.

It was born in the darkness of the Cold War when fear of great masses of Soviet armor were

As seen here in 1977, the final assembly of the Copperhead at the Martin Marietta Electronics Orlando Division included wiring and testing of electrical, optical, and gyroscope components of the laser-sensing nose that guided the 155-mm projectile. *Martin Marietta*

A tank is about to die. The SMAW Mk.153 launcher includes the fiberglass/epoxy launch tube, the spotting rifle mounted on the right side of the launch tube, and a firing mechanism that uses a magneto to fire the rocket. The encased rockets are loaded at the rear of the launcher. The spotting cartridges are stored in a magazine in the cap of the encased rocket. *McDonnell Douglas*

Hellfire

Like Copperhead, Hellfire was a guided weapon born at the depths of the Cold War as a desperate means of killing as many Soviet tanks as possible, because of the vast Soviet numeric superiority. In the 1950s, the U.S. Army imagined doing this with atomic cannons and nuclear Davy Crocketts. By the 1970s, the paradigm shift had turned from massive obliteration to making every shot count with guided weapons.

As compellingly colorful as the name Hellfire might be, it is said to have actually been adapted originally as a loosely formed acronym for the helicopter-launched fire-and-forget missile. The program began in 1971 as a study aimed at developing such a weapon. It was in 1976 that a development contract for the Hellfire was awarded. Rockwell International (part of Boeing since 1996) was awarded the initial contract, which the company ultimately shared equally with Martin Marietta (part of Lockheed Martin since 1994). After several years of testing, the Hellfire entered production in 1982.

The Martin Marietta Electronics Copperhead laser-guided artillery projectile achieved greater than 90 percent reliability in periodic test firings of production lots during 1985. *Martin Marietta*

a paramount concern for the U.S. Army as it faced the specter of World War III. Copperhead was a 137-pound high-explosive antitank round designed to be fired from a 155-mm howitzer just like any other 155-mm artillery round. It was intended to be used on the dreadful day when every shot would count.

When the Copperhead was fired, a thermal battery, timer, and gyro were activated. In flight, the Copperhead was guided by a laser designator from either a helicopter or a ground source. The designator illuminated the target, and a sensor in the nose of the Copperhead guided the missile to the laser beam on the target up to ten miles from the howitzer.

A protective harness assembly on the Copperhead guidance section is adjusted before the units leave the Orlando, Florida, production line for environmental stress tests, circa 1984. *Martin Marietta*

The control section of this Copperhead laser-guided projectile is inspected at the Martin Marietta Electronics facility at Ocala, Florida, before the shells are delivered to the U.S. Army, circa 1986. *Martin Marietta*

Through the end of the twentieth century, more than 60,000 Hellfires of all variants were built. Production continued into the twenty-first century, with all new variants except the specialized AGM-114L being delivered by Hellfire Systems, a joint venture of Boeing and Lockheed Martin.

The Hellfires all have a thirteen-inch wingspan and a diameter of seven inches. Depending on the variant and warhead, Hellfires range in length from sixty-four to seventy inches, and in weight from 100 to 110 pounds. The range is nearly two miles, and the top speed Mach 1.3.

The AGM-114 Hellfire achieved its combat success after the Cold War, with its first big baptism of fire in Gulf War I, and widespread use in Gulf War II. Designed to be used by attack helicopters, the Hellfire was adapted in the twenty-first century for use on unmanned drones, notably the MQ-1 Predator. In Yemen on November 4, 2002, a Hellfire-armed Predator took out a sport utility vehicle full of al Qaeda capos, including Qaed Senyan al-Harthi, one of the schemers who had planned the suicide attack that had damaged the USS *Cole* in Yemen twenty-five months earlier, killing seventeen Americans.

A second-generation Hellfire missile system seeker homes in on a laser-illuminated target in 1984. At that time, Martin Marietta Electronics was developing the Hellfire optimized missile system, now known as Hellfire II, which would feature an improved warhead and greater resistance to countermeasures. *Martin Marietta*

Advanced-Threat Infrared Countermeasures

A defensive system born as the Cold War faded, the advanced threat infrared countermeasures (ATIRCM) hardware would prove itself in the hostile-threat environments faced by United States forces in the early years of the twenty-first century. Both ATIRCM and the common missile warning system (CMWS) evolved toward the end of the Cold War as part of the U.S. Army's suite of integrated infrared countermeasures (SIIRCM) concept of infrared protection for helicopter use. SIIRCM also included advanced infrared countermeasures munitions (AIRCMM), a set of infrared flare decoys, and passive infrared features. These features are the host-platform modifications that are intended to reduce infrared signatures, and include such things as engine exhaust/heat suppression and infrared-absorbing paints.

The army ATIRCM program was merged with the U.S. Navy and Air Force advanced missile warning system (AMWS) program. For the U.S. Army only, the ATIRCM/CMWS was integrated with the advanced-threat radar jammer (ATRJ), a radio-frequency (RF) system, to provide overall infrared and radio-frequency self-protection.

Because of the modular design of ATIRCM/CMWS, multiple configurations were possible on a wide range of aircraft and ground vehicles. Initially, the aircraft included the army's MH-60 helicopters, marine corps AV-8B Harriers, and air force F-16s, but the army later included it on

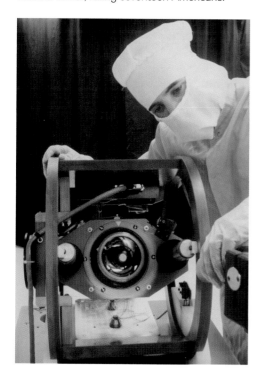

The surface of a Hellfire missile's target seeker, which reflects a laser beam, is examined during rigorous quality control tests at Martin Marietta Electronics in Orlando, Florida, in 1984. *Martin Marietta*

A total of 18,328 Hellfires had been delivered by the end of 1990, when this picture was taken. Flight tests during that year brought the record to 202 direct hits in 203 firings. Three months later, the Hellfire was in action in Gulf War I. *Martin Marietta*

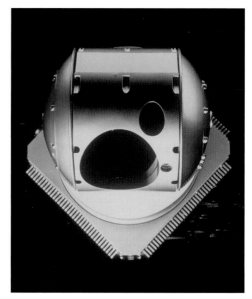

By 1995, the Lockheed Sanders advanced tactical infrared countermeasures (ATIRCM) system was integrated with the U.S. Navy and Air Force advanced missile warning system (AMWS) program. *Lockheed Martin*

many models of MH-47 Chinook and OH-58 Kiowa helicopters, as well as AH-64D Apache attack choppers.

AV-8B Night-Attack Systems

In late 1987 and early 1988, McDonnell Douglas and the U.S. Marine Corps began introducing the night-attack variant of the AV-8B Harrier II aircraft. We mention this program because it's typical of the technological upgrades that accompanied the microprocessor revolution of the 1980s and which transformed electronic systems at every level. Turning night into day for Harrier drivers was just a small part of how this would transform the United States military during the last decade of the Cold War.

Several new systems built into the Night Attack AV-8B included a forward looking infrared

The early Lockheed Sanders advanced tactical infrared countermeasures (ATIRCM) system is seen in this 1993 photograph. It was destined to be the infrared countermeasures system for U.S. Army helicopters and fixed-wing aircraft. *Lockheed Martin*

This pilot of a Night Attack–configured AV-8B Harrier II, seen here at China Lake in April 1988, looks like the central casting image of someone from a late-twentieth-century science fiction film. *McDonnell Douglas*

(FLIR) sensor and a color digital moving map display. New night-vision goggles for the pilot were complemented with new cockpit lighting that was compatible with the goggles. The AV-8B Night Attack program took place at the China Lake Naval Weapons Center in California as well as at the Naval Air Test Center at Patuxent River, Maryland, and remote sites within Camp Lejeune, North Carolina, where the aircraft operated at night from two-lane roads.

According to Jack Jackson, program test pilot for the McDonnell Aircraft component of McDonnell Douglas, the airplane's new weapons-delivery system has demonstrated accuracy equal to that possible in daylight. "We've worked on integrating the new goggles, [and] moving map and infrared sensors into the airplane's existing avionics suite," said Jackson, who took part in the 1988 test program along with Marine Corps pilots. "This isn't a matter of improving existing capabilities. These are operations that wouldn't be done at all now [were it not for the night-attack improvements]. A plane like the Night Attack AV-8B, with its basing flexibility, will revolutionize the battlefield concept and ease the combat environment for the rifleman on the ground."

The first production Night Attack Harrier II was delivered early in 1989, and in June of that year, VMF-214, the Black Sheep Squadron of World War II fame, became the Marine Corps' first AV-8B Night Attack Squadron.

Stealth Warships

The development of stealth technology was one of the most important breakthroughs in weapons systems in the 1980s. At that time, it was applied only to aircraft, specifically to the Lockheed F-117 Nighthawk stealth fighter and the Northrop B-2 Spirit stealth bomber. In the 1990s, Lockheed announced that it had taken the technology a step further with the world's first stealth warship.

The once supersecret stealth technology is actually a group of technologies designed to absorb or deflect radar to render an aircraft virtually invisible. To create such an aircraft, designers had first studied the nature of radar. For instance, radar doesn't perceive size, only contour, shape, and surface. A glossy, light-colored surface reflects light and also reflects radar back

to its receiver, so to defeat radar, designers would paint the airplane with a flat dark radar-absorbing paint. Metallic surfaces also reflect radar, so the use of a nonmetallic plastic material like Kevlar would go a long way toward reducing radar detectability.

Efforts that led to stealth aircraft began in the mid-1970s within the Defense Advanced Research Projects Agency (DARPA) and the U.S. Air Force with the supersecret air-to-surface technology evaluation and integration (ASTEI) program and the covert survivable in-weather reconnaissance/strike (CSIRS) program. The

Like nothing you have ever encountered at sea! The *Sea Shadow* (IX-529) is seen here during sea trials in the Pacific Ocean, circa 1990. *Lockheed Missiles & Space*

The *Sea Shadow* (IX-529) emerges from its lair, the Hughes Mining Barge, moored at Redwood City, California, circa 1993. *Lockheed Missiles & Space*

Passing under the San Francisco Bay Bridge with the city's skyline in the background, circa 1993, the *Sea Shadow* (IX-529) stealth warship elicited numerous glances from the curious. *Lockheed Missiles & Space*

technology was ultimately implemented in operational aircraft both by the Northrop Corporation and by Lockheed's Advanced Developments Projects office, known informally as the Skunk Works.

The stealth warship was a joint project of DARPA, the navy, and Lockheed Missiles & Space Company. It was in progress while Lockheed was at work on the F-117, which made its first flight in June 1981 at the Groom Lake test facility north of Nellis Air Force Base in Nevada (once known as Area 51). The result of the stealth warship project was the ship known as Sea Shadow (IX-529), which had an appearance unlike any military ship ever seen. It incorporated the small water plane area twin hull (SWATH) design, in which the hull, which looked somewhat like the forward fuselage of the F-117, was suspended above the water on angled pontoons. The faceted, flat black surface of the Sea Shadow was completely smooth, because any protruding antenna or weapon would dramatically increase the radar signature.

The secret vessel was constructed inside the huge Hughes Mining Barge (HMB-1), moored at Redwood City, California, near the Lockheed Missiles & Space Company headquarters at Sunnyvale. Supersecret sea trials were conducted in San Francisco Bay and in the Pacific only at night. The ship slipped under the Golden Gate Bridge in the moonless darkness and returned to its lair inside the Hughes Mining

Barge—like a character in a Hollywood vampire movie—before daylight.

The Sea Shadow was powered by a diesel electric engine with a twin-screw diesel electronic drive. It was 164 feet long, with a beam of 68 feet, a draft of 14.5 feet, and a displacement of 560 tons. It was designed to be operated by a crew of eight to ten. During testing, the ship was generally manned by a specialized crew from Lockheed (Lockheed-Martin since 1994), though onboard combat systems such as the automated combat identification system (ACIDS) and the tactical action advisor (TAA) were almost certainly manned by U.S. Navy personnel.

The U.S. Navy finally officially revealed the existence of the strange ship in April 1993, as daylight testing of the Sea Shadow began off the coast of Southern California. Both the Sea Shadow and the Hughes Mining Barge were relocated to a new home port at Naval Station San Diego by the end of 1994. By this time, the Sea Shadow had already been integrated into naval battle group exercises.

In 1999, the ship was being used to provide a test platform for technology that the U.S. Navy hoped to incorporate into its DD-21 twenty-first-century land-attack destroyer development program. Once again based in San Francisco Bay, the Sea Shadow took part in the Third Fleet's Battle Experiment Echo in 1999 and Battle Experiment Hotel in 2000. The Sea Shadow was also used for DARPA's high-performance distributed experiment (HiPer-D) program.

Some of the low-observable technology pioneered by the Sea Shadow design has also been incorporated into the recent Arleigh Burke–class destroyers. Having been aboard such ships, the author has noted that many of the bulkhead surfaces that are traditionally vertical are now slanted, a method for helping to deflect radar. Meanwhile, the vessel's SWATH technology has been adapted for the somewhat more conventional Victorious and Impeccable classes of T-AGOS ocean-surveillance ships.

The Strategic Defense Initiative

In the history of twentieth-century weapons systems, the decade of the 1980s will always be remembered as the decade of Star Wars, although the technology that the term describes has its roots in the 1950s. Essentially, Star Wars developed the concept of anti-ballistic-missile (ABM) systems. The premise is rudimentary. It takes no stretch of imagination to perceive intercontinental ballistic missiles armed with thermonuclear weapons as the most terrible of weapons. It also is not taxing to the imagination to suppose that the potential victims of an attack by such weapons would want to defend themselves.

In the 1960s, the United States anti-ballistic-missile programs, specifically Project Sentinel and Project Safeguard, were headed by the U.S. Army and were a direct extension of the army's responsibility for ground-based air defense. The United States built a single ABM site under Project Safeguard. Located in North Dakota to defend the ICBM fields on the northern plains, it contained thirty Spartan missile silos and seventy launch sites for shorter-range Sprint missiles. This complex was activated in April 1975, but the United States Congress abruptly took the unexpected step of ordering the Ford administration to deactivate the site almost as soon as it became fully operational. The Soviet Union, meanwhile, went on to build an elaborate ABM system to defend Moscow.

By 1983, the United States was essentially defenseless against a Soviet ICBM attack, while the Soviet Union had a relatively sophisticated, albeit partial, missile defense system

that had been in place for a decade. The only defense that the United States had was the threat of massive retaliation under the old doctrine of mutual assured destruction (MAD). In his famous address to the nation on March 23, 1983, President Ronald Reagan proposed superseding MAD with a defensive system. In his speech, Reagan decried "deterrence of aggression through the promise of retaliation," and asked rhetorically whether it might be "better to save lives than to avenge them? Are we not capable of demonstrating our peaceful intentions by applying all our abilities and our ingenuity to achieving a truly lasting stability?" Ultimately, Reagan's decision to undertake the SDI achieved that stability—if not globally, at least across all of Europe,

A 1987 Martin Marietta Astronautics artist's rendering depicts the Zenith Star space-based laser station. Key elements proposed included a chemical laser, a sophisticated mirror system, high-power optics, and advanced tracking and pointing. *Martin Marietta*

Los Alamos National Laboratory technicians are shown working on the field-reverse laser-energy project, one of many SDI programs, circa 1986. *LANL photo*

Here we see a 1986 evaluation of a laser rapid retargeting and precision pointing (R2P2) system for SDI applications at the Martin Marietta Astronautics laboratory in Denver. This lab provided a unique national test facility for ground or space systems requiring highly accurate pointing capabilities, such as space telescopes, space-station instruments, and lasers for communications. *Martin Marietta*

The compact toroid laser at the Los Alamos National Laboratory, during the SDI era, circa 1986. A laser can be emitted to the inside of a very big transparent toroid filled with a reactive gas. A toroid is a doughnut-shaped object. *LANL photo*

The Los Alamos National Laboratory's radio frequency linear accelerator, circa 1986. *LANL photo*

the theater in which World War III was long expected to occur.

The post-1983 ABM program, known as the Strategic Defense Initiative (SDI), was managed by the Strategic Defense Initiative Organization (SDIO) at the Department of Defense and received input from all of the armed services. Technologically, SDI differed greatly from the Project Safeguard–era systems. Under Safeguard, a nuclear warhead would have been used in an effort to destroy everything within a given blast radius. The SDI concept was to combine a conventional warhead with a better guidance system to "hit a bullet with a bullet."

The Strategic Defense Initiative Organization focused on a wide variety of non-nuclear systems. These ranged from lasers and particle beams to kinetic kill vehicles (KKV) that would have destroyed targets through the use of non-explosive projectiles moving at very high speeds.

Ultimately, even though they were never operationally deployed, the weapons of the Strategic Defense Initiative were more significant than anyone could have imagined in 1983. The scientific breakthroughs achieved by the Strategic Defense Initiative Organization presented such a technological challenge to the Soviet war machine that they are now credited with being among the most important weapons in winning the Cold War.

Homing Overlay Experiment

One of the first of the new-generation systems to be tested by the Strategic Defense Initiative Office was the homing overlay experiment (HOE). Designed and built by the Lockheed Missiles & Space Company, HOE was a kinetic-energy weapon funded jointly by the Strategic Defense Initiative Organization and the U.S. Army's Ballistic Missile Defense Systems Command. It was designed to use a unique system of unfurlable fan blades to increase its ability to hit a target.

For test purposes, the HOE homing and killer module was attached as the upper stage of a Minuteman ICBM. It included long-wavelength infrared-detection and -homing techniques for in-flight guidance to the target. Prior to contact with the target, the interceptor would unfurl the "fan"—a metal ribbed-array structure with a diameter of about thirteen feet. Because of the closing speed of the two objects, there was no need for an explosive device on the interceptor. Just the collision would be lethal to the target.

There were four tests of the HOE system, all launched from the Kwajalein missile range. In each, a Minuteman target missile was launched from Vandenberg Air Force Base in California on a flight path that closely resembled the trajectory of an intercontinental ballistic missile. The course of the missile took it west over the Pacific. For reference, Kwajalein is in the Marshall Island chain, more than four thousand miles away from the launch site in California. While the unarmed ICBM was on its trajectory, the interceptor was launched, and it accelerated to a speed of more than ten thousand miles per hour. When the radar at Kwajalein acquired the target, the interceptor was directed toward it and given final automatic control of the intercept.

The first three tests, between February and December 1983, involved successful launches, but there were interceptor failures due to software and sensor glitches. On June 10, 1984, an HOE successfully intercepted a target ICBM. When the two missiles made contact at an altitude of about ninety miles above the Pacific, they had a combined closing speed of about 5.5 miles per second (almost twenty thousand miles per hour), and the force of the impact destroyed both missiles. Telemetry data showed that the intercept was nose to nose.

Of the test, deputy assistant Secretary of the Army Amoretta Hoeber said, "We tried to hit a bullet with a bullet and it worked." The intercept of the ICBM by the HOE was quite significant for defense-system planners. It showed that the technology was available to kill offensive threats in the late-boost through midcourse phases of a ballistic missile trajectory. The precision of the event was particularly impressive. The apparent success of the homing overlay experiment won Lockheed the 1986 Strategic Defense Technical Achievement Award.

However, a 1993 report in The New York Times insinuated that the successful test nine years earlier had actually been faked in order to fool the Soviet Union, the United States Congress, or both. It was said that the target missile was equipped with a transponder on which the HOE interceptor could have "homed." In fact, transponders are a standard safety precaution to prevent the test missiles from getting lost and hitting an unintended target, and a device capable of homing on the transponder would have been too large for the HOE to have carried. The successful test was almost certainly not faked.

Krypton Fluoride Laser

One of the little-known SDI projects undertaken by the Los Alamos National Laboratory in New Mexico during the 1980s involved the use of

krypton fluoride excimer lasers. By definition, excimer lasers are pulsed-gas lasers that produce high-energy pulses in the ultraviolet portion of the spectrum. These lasers use a mix of a rare gases such as argon, xenon, or krypton, along with a halide gas, such as chlorine or fluorine, in an intense, transverse discharge to create an excimer, short for excited dimer, a molecule that only exists in an excited state, such as argon fluoride, xenon chloride, or krypton fluoride.

According to the Naval Research Laboratory, a high-voltage pulsed-power source generates a uniform electron beam from the cathode. The electron beam propagates through the foil support and deposits its energy in the laser cell, filled with krypton, fluorine, and argon gases. A complex set of ionizations and chemical reactions produces the excited molecular state of krypton fluoride. The input laser beam then stimulates the decay of this molecule to its ground state of separate atoms, with an enhancement of the laser intensity.

The strange-looking homing overlay experiment (HOE) interceptor vehicle was certainly unique. It was designed with a ribbed array of unfurlable fan blades that increased its diameter to thirteen feet. This illustration depicts the mission on June 10, 1984, when an HOE successfully intercepted its target at a speed of twenty-thousand miles per hour. *Lockheed Missiles & Space*

The powerful krypton fluoride laser known as Aurora is in place at the Los Alamos National Laboratory, circa 1986. Imagine such a machine as part of an orbiting battle station. *LANL photo*

Technicians are at work on the krypton fluoride laser during SDI experiments conducted at the Los Alamos National Laboratory, circa 1986. The Naval Research Laboratory has reported that krypton fluoride lasers have demonstrated outstanding beam uniformity. *LANL photo*

While excimer lasers are relatively straight-forward mechanisms, they are very complex. This is a result of the corrosive character of the halide gasses and the need to maintain a cool, homogeneous blend of gas in the area of the discharge. Originally considered merely as research tools, excimer lasers eventually found practical applications in the semiconductor industry and in ophthalmology for photorefractive keratectomy—and potential applications in missile defense.

BEAR

Originating at the Los Alamos National Laboratory, the beam experiment aboard rocket (BEAR) accelerator is reported to have been part of an SDI experiment to demonstrate the operation of an ion accelerator in space, and to

Loaded for bear, the beam experiment aboard rocket is seen here at Los Alamos in June 1989. A month later, it would be launched from the White Sands Missile Range, recovered, and returned to the laboratory. *Author's collection*

characterize the exoatmospheric propagation of a neutral particle beam. The BEAR incorporated a radio-frequency quadrapole that was operated under power with the beam in the laboratory. The BEAR, with its functioning accelerator, was successfully launched on July 13, 1989. During the flight, the neutral hydrogen beam was successfully operated outside the earth's atmosphere. After the flight, the BEAR was recovered by parachute with minor damage and operated again in the laboratory.

ERIS

Using the technical knowledge base developed during the Homing Overlay Experiment, the Lockheed Missiles & Space Company undertook work on the exoatmospheric reentry vehicle interceptor system (ERIS), also developed for the U.S. Army, as well as the Strategic Defense Initiative Office. The ERIS system was similar to HOE, but it utilized more advanced technology and was a much lighter kill vehicle. Like the high

An eerie glow from the krypton fluoride laser at the Los Alamos National Laboratory, circa 1986. Such lasers are known for their generation of bright, extreme-ultraviolet harmonic radiation. *LANL photo*

The first operational Lockheed Missiles & Space Company exoatmospheric reentry vehicle interceptor system (ERIS) at Kwajalein Island in early 1991. *Lockheed Martin*

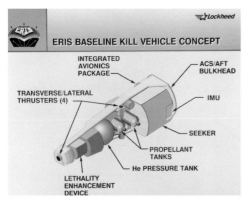

This March 1987 cutaway illustration details the components of the exoatmospheric reentry vehicle interceptor system (ERIS). The integrated avionics package (IAP) computer (top left) receives interceptor vehicle position data from the onboard inertial measurement unit (IMU) and target data from the seeker. The seeker acquires and tracks the incoming warhead. The IAP sends guidance commands to the two transverse and two lateral thrusters. The thrusters, powered by liquid propellants, jockey the ERIS vehicle to the impact point. Helium is used to pressurize the fuel tanks and as a propellant for the altitude control system (ACS) at the aft bulkhead. The lethality enhancement device would deploy just before impact to provide a larger hit area. *Lockheed Missiles & Space*

endoatmospheric defense interceptor (HEDI), which is described in more detail later, ERIS used a thrust-vector system for attitude control during boost phase (the early part of the missile's trajectory, when the missile is pushing against gravity). The inter-stage at the forward end of the booster contained a separation motor to ensure the kill vehicle's separation. The guidance system utilized data from midcourse sensors to allow ERIS to hit its target.

Early testing began in 1989, and the first publicly acknowledged successful intercept of a dummy warhead by ERIS occurred in January 1991, as the Cold War was coming to a close. A second test a year later was also successful, but the system was mothballed because of the end of the Cold War. The technology embodied within it was later adapted for the theater high-altitude area defense (THAAD) system, a ground-based missile defense system that was first tested in 1995 and earmarked for deployment by 2010.

On January 28, 1991, this exoatmospheric reentry vehicle interceptor system (ERIS) was launched from Kwajalein Island, successfully intercepting an Aries sounding rocket. A second launch on March 13, 1992, against a Minuteman was also a success. *Lockheed Martin*

This artist's conception of a hypervelocity railgun, circa 1986, looks like something from a *Star Wars* movie. Maybe that's why the media loved to refer to the Strategic Defense Initiative as "Star Wars." *SDIO*

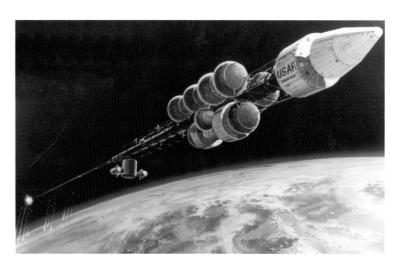

Radio frequency quadrapole technology was just one of many avenues explored at the Los Alamos National Laboratory during the 1980s in an effort to develop a practical SDI railgun capable of destroying enemy ballistic missiles. Advanced forms of similar technology are at play in current railgun experiments. *LANL photo*

Railguns

Theorized before the First World War, the concept of utilizing a system of electromagnets to launch projectiles fascinated weapons designers throughout the twentieth century, and such weapons are still being studied. Railguns would have very high muzzle velocities, thereby reducing the lead angle required to shoot down fast-moving objects. If the guns were fired in the atmosphere, this fast muzzle velocity would flatten trajectories. (Originally electromagnetic guns were conceived of only as a ground-based weapon because of the extreme electrical power requirements. In the 1980s, scientists began studying ways to develop sufficient power to base the guns in space.)

Modern hypervelocity railguns work very much like a nuclear particle accelerator. A metal pellet (the projectile) is attracted down a guide (the rail) of magnetic fields and accelerated by the rapid on-off switching of the various fields. The hypersonic speeds attained by these small projectiles are dazzling.

Under SDI, hypervelocity railguns were, at least conceptually, seen as an attractive alternative for a space-based defense system. This is because of their envisioned ability to quickly shoot many projectiles at many targets. Unlike larger kinetic weapons such as missiles, the system would be cheaper to operate. As with a conventional gun, only a relatively inexpensive projectile is expended.

During the 1960s, the Soviet Union developed an experimental gun that could shoot streams of particles of heavy metals, such as tungsten or molybdenum, at speeds of nearly fifteen miles per second in air and more than thirty-six miles per second in a vacuum. In one experiment

conducted by the Strategic Defense Initiative Office during the 1980s, a small particle was accelerated to a velocity of more than twenty-four miles per second. (At that speed, the projectile could circle the earth at the equator in something less than twenty minutes.) Two decades later, the compact high-energy capacitor module advanced-technology experiment (CHECMATE) managed by the Strategic Defense Initiative Organization, was prepared during the mid-1980s to conduct an extensive railgun test program.

One of the major technical challenges faced in operating a railgun system is the acceleration of the projectile. At the speeds mentioned above, the acceleration stresses the pellet to pressures in excess of one hundred thousand times the normal force of gravity. In more popular terms, the acceleration of the pellet can be expressed in terms of one hundred thousand G's. A G is the acceleration of an object that is acted upon by gravity. As a passenger of a modern jetliner, you are pushed into your seat at takeoff by two Gs of acceleration, and six to nine Gs are felt by fighter pilots in top-performance aircraft. On the average, humans tend to black out at about ten Gs.

Even with this limited view of G forces, it is easy to understand that the jolt of explosive acceleration in a railgun could easily tear the projectile apart. In order to be effective, the projectile must be able to withstand the initial acceleration in order to get to the target.

Another challenge with the railgun is the stress the rapid firing of the gun places on the rails. In order to rapidly accelerate the pellet, the rail must rapidly switch its magnetic fields on and

A Los Alamos National Laboratory technician is at work with a neutral particle beam SDI experiment, circa 1986. Such hardware was envisioned as leading to a prototype of an operational SDI system. *LANL Photo*

Considered as a possible prototype for an SDI space-based particle-beam battle station was the integrated space experiment system (ISES), seen here on terra firma in December 1987. *Author's collection*

off. This extremely fast switching requires a tremendous current of electricity (almost half a million amps) to pass through the rails every time the gun is fired. In some experiments, the rails had to be replaced after each firing.

Finally, there is the desire to install a sensor or homing device in larger railgun projectiles. Such a projectile would need to be hardened to keep its shape, and the electronics inside it would need to be able to function after being stressed by the initial acceleration.

At the end of the twentieth century, railguns were still only a step this side of science fiction. But today they have the potential to become an integral part of the high-technology defensive arsenal.

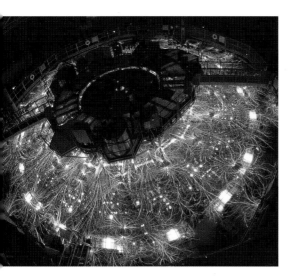

A particle-beam fusion accelerator at the Sandia National Laboratory in New Mexico, circa 1993. *Lockheed Martin*

Particle-Beam Weapons

As with lasers, particle beams conjure up notions of early-twentieth-century pulp-science-fiction death rays. By definition, particle-beam weapons are systems that rely on the technology of particle accelerators to emit beams of charged or neutral subatomic particles, which travel at nearly the speed of light. Such a beam could theoretically destroy a target by several means, including electronic disruption, softening of metal, and explosive destruction.

As a laser uses amplified light, a neutral particle beam could use accelerated negative ions as a disruptive energy force. These weapons differ from kinetic kill vehicles (KKV) in that they use energy beams rather than tangible projectiles.

The science behind neutral-particle-beam weapons originated with experiments conducted in the Soviet Union in the 1960s. Indeed, the Soviet scientific literature included extensive articles about their research efforts that were conducted well before the American Strategic Defense Initiative. Apparently, the Soviets became aware of the potential weapons applications of the research in the early 1970s, when they suddenly stopped reporting on this sensitive subject in international scientific journals.

Under the Strategic Defense Initiative Office, neutral-particle-beam weapons were envisioned as being configured much like the space-based lasers. A series of these weapons could have been placed in an orbital network, where they could have been capable of engaging ballistic missile boosters and post-boost rockets as their launch trajectories lifted them out of the atmosphere.

This artist's conception, circa 1986, shows a pair of space-based SDI neutral particle beam weapons shooting down incoming Soviet ICBMs at the apogee of their trajectories. It would take fast action to defeat a salvo launch such as seen here. Although designed as a weapons system, the space-based particle beam stations could also provide a sensor function for the defense system during the post-boost and midcourse phases of a missile trajectory. It appears that when an object is "hit" by a particle beam, it emits gamma rays and neutrons. The gamma rays and neutrons released were possibly in proportion to the size and mass of the object. With this in mind, these emissions could be used to discriminate between lightweight decoys and heavier reentry vehicles. *LANL artist concept*

At Martin Marietta Astronautics, Denver, engineers discuss miniaturization of this engineering model of a Brilliant Pebbles spacecraft, circa 1991. *Martin Marietta*

A Brilliant Pebbles test vehicle hovers under its own power, controlled by microbursts from its rocket engines, during a 1989 SDI demonstration at Edwards Air Force Base. The demo showed the ability of the seeker and an image processor to distinguish a missile from its rocket-exhaust plume. *Martin Marietta*

Such a particle-beam weapon could disable a missile without actually destroying it. The beam of charged particles would not burn a hole in the skin of a missile as would a laser beam. Instead, the particle beam would easily pass through the skin of a missile and disrupt the electronic devices on board.

More importantly, neutral particle beams offer the promise of efficiently destroying enemy intercontinental ballistic missiles during their

boost phase. SDI planners were interested in the fact that particle-beam weapons have an unlimited stream of energy. Because of this (and the fact that the beams penetrate through the target), these weapons do not need to dwell on targets as lasers do.

Particle-beam technology could also provide the same destructive punch as lasers. Depending on what sort of particles are used (there are many choices: electrons, protons, or hydrogen atoms), the beam can strike a physical blow as well as an electronic impact. The physical force would be quite destructive because of the near-light-speed velocity of the beam. It could be that particle-beam weapons of the future will have the capability of either physically destroying a target or disabling it by way of electronic disruption.

In the late 1980s, Strategic Defense Initiative Office scientists developed and successfully tested the radio-frequency quadrapole pre-accelerator, which accelerates a charged beam. This development is considered a major improvement in particle-beam technology. Experiments also produced an ion beam with qualities superior to SDI design goals.

In the final years of the Cold War, the neutral particle beam technology integration experiment investigated the technologies needed to perform midcourse discrimination or to detect nuclear material. This experiment was conducted in space at low power levels and used nearby co-orbital instrumented targets.

Brilliant Pebbles and Brilliant Eyes

One of the most promising kinetic energy projects studied by the Strategic Defense Initiative Organization was a system that used swarms of small, lightweight interceptor projectiles. Code-named Brilliant Pebbles, this weapon envisioned about 4,600 small interceptors that would be deployed in orbit 288 miles above the earth for a period of ten years. Because there would have been so many, the Brilliant Pebbles galaxy would have been effectively invulnerable to any imaginable Soviet anti-satellite weapon. Brilliant Pebbles was to have been supported by a system of fifty tracking-sensor satellites developed under the code name Brilliant Eyes.

The pebbles were one-hundred-pound weapons capsules that were brilliant because

This illustration showing the various components of the Brilliant Pebbles interceptor was released in March 1990. *SDIO*

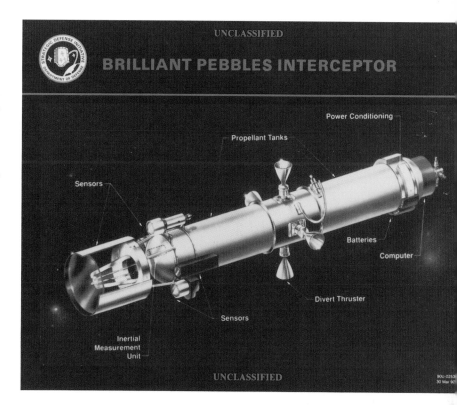

each would carry a sensor and would be capable of operating independently from other pebbles or any external guidance or control system. The system would be inert until activated, but when triggered by a human operator, each pebble would be capable of tracking the infrared signature of an ICBM at its most vulnerable—during the boost phase—computing the trajectory, plotting an intercept course, and destroying the incoming hostile warhead.

During July and August 1988, President Reagan was personally briefed on Brilliant Pebbles by Lawrence Livermore National Laboratory physicists, including Edward Teller, the father of the United States hydrogen bomb. In February 1990, the Strategic Defense Initiative Organization was ready to issue the contracts to actually start building Brilliant Pebbles. The prime contractor was the Space Transportation Systems Division of Rockwell International (a component of the Boeing Company after 1996), then located in Downey, in suburban Los Angeles. The second source contractor was the Martin Marietta campus in Denver, Colorado (now Lockheed Martin Strategic and Space Systems).

The program was seen as the technological breakthrough that had been hoped for since 1983, a reasonably low-cost missile-defense system that could have been in place by the turn of the century. With an estimated price tag of $55.3 billion to develop and deploy, Brilliant Pebbles was actually inexpensive by comparison to the other programs then being considered.

After promising early experiments in 1989, Martin Marietta and Thompson Ramo Woolridge (TRW) were given pre-full-scale development contracts for Brilliant Pebbles and Brilliant Eyes in June 1991. They are recalled as having been the first SDI programs to officially make the transition from experimental projects to major defense acquisition programs.

The Strategic Defense Initiative Organization was planning for an initial deployment of the Brilliant Pebbles system between 1994 and 1996, but this was put on ice with the end of

the Cold War. Late in the decade, however, the Ballistic Missile Defense Organization revisited national missile defense under the Global Protection Against Limited Strikes (GPALS) doctrine. Brilliant Pebbles was brought in from the cold. Brilliant Eyes was also revived, and at the turn of the century, it was under development by TRW (a part of Northrop Grumman after 2002) as the space-based infrared system (SBIRS).

Work on the Brilliant Pebbles program progressed to assembly and testing at the Martin Marietta Electronics facility at Orlando, Florida, in 1992. The developmental spacecraft would be delivered to Kwajalein for launch the following year. *Martin Marietta*

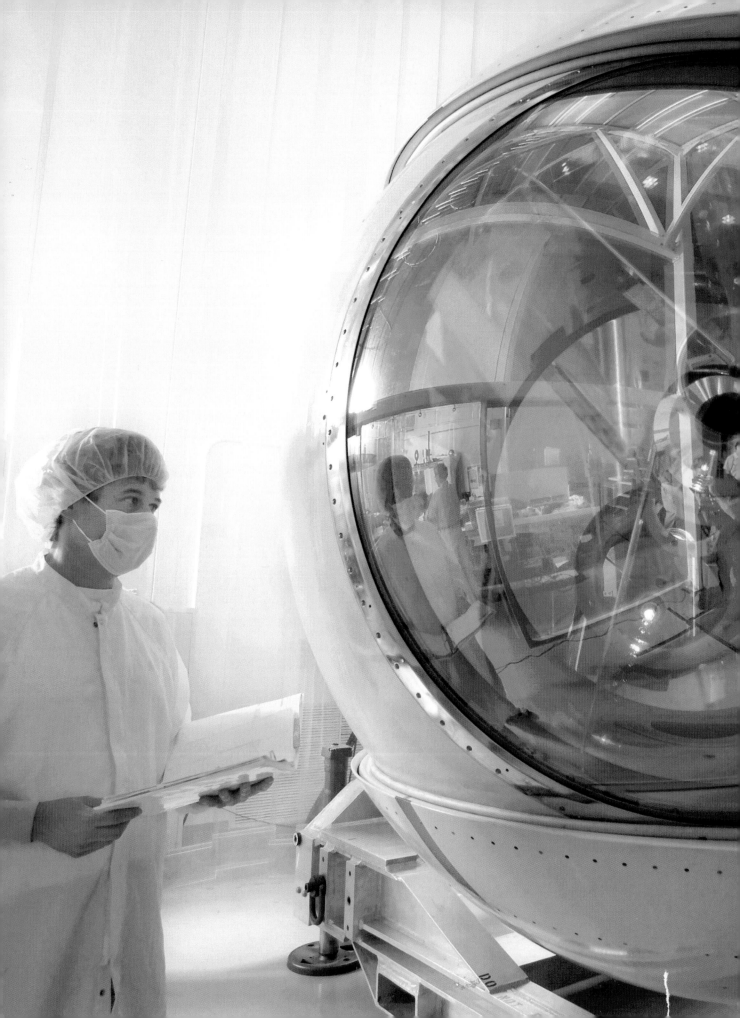

CHAPTER FOUR

INTO THE
TWENTY-FIRST
CENTURY

The history and evolution of warfare and weapons systems changed more dramatically in the final years of the Cold War than it had since the end of World War II. As in civilian life, the advent of unimaginably smaller and smaller, and faster and faster, microprocessors made things possible in the 1990s that could not have been conceived at the end of the 1970s.

In terms of military applications, however, the end of the Cold War brought an interlude of technological retrenchment. Ends of long wars are typically accompanied by sighs of relief and momentary euphoria. This feeling of well-being soon fades when we realize that the end of a war does not mean peace. Even as the Cold War ended, messianic madmen were already crawling out from dark, dank holes in Southwest Asia and elsewhere to menace the world with new threats.

As the world crossed the threshold of a new millennium, threats arose from stateless bandits and a disjointed collection of rogue states that included those nations that President George W. Bush once referred to as the Axis of Evil—Iraq, Iran, and North Korea. The specific threats

ranged from low-tech savagery to weapons of mass destruction.

The gadgets and gear developed by and for the United States arsenal since the late 1990s has been as varied as at any time in history. The systems discussed in this chapter represent a randomly selected wide variety. Some of the common themes come from a new generation of smart munitions and projectiles, as well as lasers that streak to their targets at the speed of light to melt metal and destroy both ballistic missiles and much smaller projectiles. Also included are such widely varied systems as defensive sensing mechanisms, an inflatable hospital, and a new family of surface vehicles that operate without a crew onboard.

The full potential of many of these systems is not yet known, but among them may well be the weapons that will one day define the course of warfare later in the twenty-first century.

The Mother of All Bombs

When deposed Iraqi dictator Saddam Hussein confidently predicted his victory in Gulf War I in 1991, he described the impending conflict as

Above: The "mother of all bombs" is prepared for her initial March 11, 2003, test at the Air Force Armament Center at Eglin Air Force Base. At the time of this writing, the precision-guided GBU-43 massive ordnance air blast (MOAB) weapon was the largest non-nuclear munition in existence. It was thirty feet long with a diameter of 40.5 inches, and it weighed just short of ten tons. *Department of Defense*

Opposite page: A Lockheed Martin Space Systems engineer in the company's Sunnyvale, California, facility inspects the turret ball conformal window on the flight turret assembly for the YAL-1A airborne laser. The window is the exit for the high-energy laser and exit and return window for the beacon illuminator and tracker illuminator lasers. *Lockheed Martin*

A Have Lite precision-guided missile is mounted on the wing pylon of a U.S. Air Force F-16. This weapon is produced by Precision Guided Systems United States (PGSUS) of Orlando, Florida. *Lockheed Martin .*

the "mother of all battles." In 2003, on the eve of his losing his second of two Gulf Wars, Saddam faced a weapon that the United States military sarcastically described as the "mother of all bombs." Though Saddam's regular forces collapsed before this weapon could be used against them, it remains the largest non-nuclear ordnance in the U.S. arsenal.

Technically, the mother of all bombs is the GBU-43 massive ordnance air blast bomb. The

acronym MOAB is applicable to either appellation. The GBU-43 is a large, powerful, and accurately deliverable weapon developed by the U.S. Air Force in just nine weeks. Weighing 27,100 pounds, the GBU-43 is the successor to the 15,000-pound BLU-82 Daisy Cutter fuel-air-explosive bomb used in Vietnam, Gulf War I, and in Afghanistan.

By comparison, the largest conventional bombs ever used in combat during the twentieth century were the British Grand Slam "Earthquake Bombs," which were used during World War II. These weapons weighed 22,000 pounds, were 26.5 feet long, and 46 inches in diameter. The MOAB is 30 feet long, with a diameter of 40.5 inches. Whereas the Grand Slam contained 9,135 pounds of Torpex high explosive, the MOAB contains 18,700 pounds of an undisclosed high explosive. The active ingredient in the BLU-82 was a slurry of ammonium nitrate, aluminum powder, and polystyrene that was exploded above ground level, producing a blast with one thousand pounds per square inch of pressure at ground zero and consuming the oxygen present in the blast area.

Both the BLU-82 and GBU-43 are delivered by transport aircraft because of the huge size of their aft cargo aperture. In Vietnam it was the C-130 Hercules, and currently the U.S. Air

An Eglin Air Force Base F-16 releases a Have Lite weapon. The base is home to the Air Force's Air Armament Center, the umbrella organization for the Precision Strike System Program Office that manages Have Lite. *Lockheed Martin*

Force uses the MC-130 Combat Talon, a special-missions variant of the Hercules. The GBU-43 is deployed on a pallet from the carrier aircraft and descends on a parachute using an inertial navigation system and global positioning system data for direction, and wings and grid fins for guidance control.

The U.S. Air Force Air Armament Center at Eglin Air Force Base conducted the initial live-fire air-launch tests of the MOAB, using an MC-130E Combat Talon I aircraft flown by a crew assigned to Eglin's 46th Test Wing. The first test was held on March 11, 2003, just before the beginning of Operation Iraqi Freedom, and the second test took place eight months later, on November 21.

In describing the initial MOAB test, Defense Secretary Donald Rumsfeld said, "The goal is to have the pressure be so great that Saddam Hussein cooperates. Short of that—an unwillingness to cooperate—the goal is to have the capabilities of the coalition so clear and so obvious that there is an enormous disincentive for the Iraqi military to fight against the coalition."

Have Lite

Imagine a missile so accurate that a building's doorway is a reasonable target, and you have the Have Lite. In the 1990s, the U.S. Air Force developed a version of the Israeli Rafael Popeye air-to-ground precision-guided missile under a program known as Have Nap. The actual missile developed under Have Nap was designated as AGM-142 and known variously as Popeye I or Raptor. The idea behind this program was a medium-range conventional standoff missile to be used by B-52s to attack high-value fixed targets. Meanwhile, Israel exported Popeye to both Turkey and Australia. For the United States, the AGM-142s were manufactured by Precision Guided Systems United States (PGSUS) of Orlando, Florida, a joint venture of Rafael in Israel and Lockheed Martin in the United States.

By the late 1990s, there was an interest in a smaller variation on Have Nap with more advanced technology for use on fighter aircraft. The result was the Have Lite program, also known as Popeye II. From a weight standpoint, Have Lite is the light version of Have Nap, although there is nothing light about its capabilities.

Making its debut early in the twenty-first century, Have Lite provides fighter aircraft such as

the F-16 and F-15E with the ability to attack and destroy high-value ground and sea targets from long range, including bunkers, power plants, missile sites, bridges, and ships—and to do so with amazing accuracy. Have Lite features include multiple guidance modes and options to provide flexible mission-planning options. It can be programmed to fly various horizontal and vertical trajectories and employs autonomous midcourse guidance based on GPS-aided inertial navigation. The missile homes in on a target using a high-performance infrared or television seeker.

Joint Direct Attack Munitions

Many of the weapons in this book illustrate the old axiom of necessity being the mother of invention. The experiences of pilots flying ground-attack missions in poor weather during Operation Desert Storm in 1991 was the catalyst for the development of a relatively inexpensive and uncomplicated way to convert existing unguided free-fall dumb bombs into accurate, adverse-weather smart munitions. The result was the joint direct attack munitions (JDAM) program. Initiated in 1992, the JDAM program led to the invention of a kit that can be attached to free-fall bombs to make them smart. This kit includes a new tail section that contains a global positioning system (GPS) and inertial navigation system (INS) for a guidance control unit.

The JDAM system entered its test phase in 1997, with both the U.S. Air Force and U.S. Navy

U.S. Air Force munitions specialists are seen working with joint direct attack munitions on the flightline during Operation Enduring Freedom in November 2001. The B-52H in the background was flying missions against the Taliban in Afghanistan. *Department of Defense*

During September 2000, the U.S. Air Force conducted tests of the joint direct attack munitions extended range (JDAM-ER). *Department of Defense*

as customers. Two years later, the JDAM was first deployed in combat during Operation Allied Force. Flying thirty-hour missions from Whiteman Air Force Base in Missouri, B-2 bombers delivered more than six hundred JDAMs against Serbian targets.

The Boeing Company created GBU-31 and GBU-32 JDAM kits for use with two-thousand-pound BLU-109 and Mk.84 bombs, as well as with one-thousand-pound BLU-110 and Mk.83 weapons. In 1999, the company introduced a JDAM kit for the Mk.82 five-hundred-pound bomb. Compatible with virtually any strike aircraft in the U.S. Air Force or U.S. Navy, the JDAM proved to be a useful system during Operation Enduring Freedom in Afghanistan as it got under way in 2001. An emergency supplemental bill, passed by Congress in late 2001, stepped up the monthly production rate of JDAMs at the Boeing factory in St. Charles, Missouri, with an eye toward an eventual total production in excess of a quarter million units.

At the time of Gulf War II in 2003, JDAM-equipped ordnance was available for use on U.S. Air Force B-1B, B-2A, B-52H, F-15E, and F-16 aircraft, as well as the navy's F-14s and late-model F/A-18 aircraft. During Operation Iraqi Freedom in the spring of 2003, 1,801 coalition aircraft dropped 18,467 smart bombs and missiles, along with 9,251 dumb bombs. Of the former total, 6,542 were JDAMs. The satellite-guided JDAM bombs proved much more effective than laser and television-guided smart weapons.

Not only is the JDAM capable of hitting fixed targets with nearly total-precision accuracy

in all weather conditions, but the weapons can be programmed en route to attack fleeting emerging targets. For example, a B-2 was able to reprogram its JDAMs on the way to Iraq to take advantage of new intelligence coming in from a Global Hawk unmanned aerial vehicle, and to launch a strike against Iraq's Republican Guard Medina Division. During Gulf War II, 22.4 percent of all munitions dropped by the U.S. Air Force were JDAMs. The air force alone plans to acquire nearly a quarter million JDAMs.

Laser-Guided Bomb Kit

As with the JDAM, the Lockheed Martin laser-guided bomb (LGB) kit is a state-of-the-art system that converts dumb gravity bombs into precision-guided munitions. The system's accuracy allows target destruction while reducing collateral damage and risks to friendly ground forces. Each guidance kit consists of a computer-control group, which is the front-end guidance system, plus an airfoil group, which includes the flight fins, which provide lift and stability. The computer control utilizes a semi-active laser seeker and pneumatically controlled guidance canards.

Paveway GBU-16 kits are used on one-thousand-pound bombs, while GBU-10 and GBU-12 kits are used on two-thousand-pound and five-hundred-pound bombs respectively. Lockheed Martin kits are compatible with the existing LGB logistics infrastructure, equipment, procedures, and aircrew operations. During Gulf

The cold-gas pneumatics of the laser-guided bomb kit guidance system eliminate the reliability and safety issues of the hot-gas system. The glass lens on the guidance system prevents the pitting that plagues plastic lenses. *Lockheed Martin*

War II, the air force dropped 8,618 LGBs, more than any other single type of ordnance, and 29.5 percent of all bombs expended by that service.

Wind-Corrected Munitions Dispenser

As with the JDAM and LGB, the wind-corrected munitions dispenser (WCMD) turns dumb bombs into smart bombs. While JDAMs are high-explosive bombs, WCMDs are cluster-bomb units. Essentially, the WCMD is an inexpensive tail-kit that transforms existing cluster munitions, such as CBU-87s, CBU-89s, and CBU-97s, into all-weather precision-guided weapons. By correcting for launch transients, ballistic errors, and winds aloft, the Lockheed Martin WCMD can give attack aircraft an accurate-pattern lay-down capability for cluster-bomb units from any operational altitude or weather condition. The air force alone plans to acquire more than 24,000 WCMDs and 7,500 extended-range WCMD-ERs. During Gulf War II, the air force used 908 WCMDs as compared to 118 CBU-87s and 182 CBU-99s.

LongShot

The phrase "smart bombs made easy" comes to mind when discussing Lockheed Martin's low-cost LongShot, a wing adaptor kit with self-contained global positioning and inertial guidance. Simply

put—and simple is the key word here—it provides any combat aircraft with the immediate ability to drop bombs from a long standoff range with affordable precision-strike capability. The system is completely self-contained, including a flight-control computer, a GPS-based navigation system, and an internal power source.

LongShot provides both range extension and autonomous guidance capability to a wide range of existing air-to-surface weapons. By using the munition's suspension lug wells as the attachment points, the kit adapts to general-purpose bombs, cluster bombs, laser-guided bombs, and sea mines. It is deployable from altitudes of five hundred to thirty-five thousand feet, up to a range of fifty nautical miles, and at night or in adverse weather.

Previous weapons required complicated military-standard smart-weapons interface systems, but these are not required with the more user-friendly LongShot, although LongShot is compatible with the older existing systems. In

Technicians examine the vanes of a wind-corrected munitions dispenser. *Lockheed Martin*

A detail view of a wind-corrected munitions dispenser. *Lockheed Martin*

A wind-corrected munitions dispenser tail unit attached to a cluster bomb unit (CBU) and ready for action. *Lockheed Martin*

LongShot provides range extension and autonomous guidance capability to a wide range of existing air-to-surface munitions in the five-hundred- and one-thousand-pound classes. The LongShot system is compatible with GBU-87, GBU-89, and GBU-97 tactical munitions dispensers. *Lockheed Martin*

other words, you don't have to be familiar with complex interfaces to use LongShot. Therefore, it is compatible with most fighter and bomber aircraft. Indeed, no aircraft modification is required to deploy a LongShot-equipped munition. Targeting information can be input via a laptop computer or through an in-aircraft kneepad device that plugs into the aircraft intercom and establishes two-way communication with LongShot via the aircraft's UHF radio. When it comes to flexibility in the heat of battle, LongShot may be one of the truly decisive weapons of the early twenty-first century.

Chemically and Biologically Protected Shelters

To allow medical staff to do their jobs during combat without concern for chemical and biological attacks, the U.S. Army deploys inflatable chemically and biologically protected shelters (CBPS). These highly mobile shelters are designed to provide a controlled, clean environment that isolates personnel from airborne contaminants for up to thirty-six hours in a chemically or biologically contaminated area.

CBPSs are carried on a Humvee and equipped with two airlocks to allow soldiers and equipment to pass in and out. Soldiers pass through the airlocks through a vertical Velcro closure in the center of each side. The airlock is purged with clean air from inside the protective shelter. A four-man crew can set up a CBPS in less than thirty minutes while dressed in chemical-protection suits rated at mission-oriented protective posture 4 (MOPP4). This means that the soldiers wear a protective suit, boots, mask, hood, and gloves.

Forward-Deployable Digital Medical Treatment Facility

Described as an operating room in a box for a combat-support hospital, the forward-deployable digital medical treatment facility (FDDMTF) is a medical technology test bed for the U.S. Army future medical shelter system (FMSS). Packed in a standard shipping container, it folds out into a structure measuring 8 by 8 by 20 feet. It was developed at the Oak Ridge National Laboratory by Duane Bias, Terry Brown, and Fariborz "Lee" Bzorgi, and had its first major

Soldiers of the U.S. Army's 3rd Infantry Division inflate a chemically and biologically protected shelter in the field in Iraq during Gulf War II in 2003. *Photo by 1st Lieutenant Michael Oliveira, 3rd Medical Command*

public demonstration at the U.S. Army Medical Materiel Development Activity (USAMMDA) at Fort Detrick, Maryland, in May 2004.

The container expands at the push of a button after the power switch is hooked up to a 24-volt battery on any standard military vehicle. The container geometrically morphs into its final shape in ninety-seven seconds. It was described by Mark Arnold, a USAMMDA engineer who had been working on the concept since 2002, as looking "like a cicada coming out." It has also

U.S. Army Major General Lester Martinez-Lopez, commander of the U.S. Army Medical Research and Materiel Command at Fort Detrick, Maryland, visited the prototype of the army's future medical shelter system on May 26, 2004. He is seen here conferring with Steve Reichard, center, and Tony Story about its future. Reichard was the program manager for the shelter program at the U.S. Army Medical Materiel Development Activity. *Department of Defense photo by Dave Rolls*

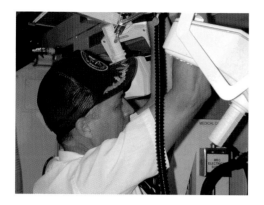

Terry Brown, an electrical engineer who worked on the future medical shelter system prototype, hangs surgical lights in the ISO container that triples in size at the push of a button. *U.S. Army photo by Karen Fleming-Michael*

Not much bigger than a dog tag, the personal information carrier may ultimately become the storage medium for a military service member's complete medical history and records. *U.S. Army Medical Research and Materiel Command*

been described as a major improvement over the then-current shelter that was packed in two ISO standard containers.

"We started with a clean sheet of paper," said Duane Bias. "It wasn't like we could take an original design and modify it to suit our needs (and) then go on and build. We spent quite a bit of time just wrestling with requirements."

The new prototype also offers users protection from chemical and biological agents, something previous systems didn't offer without extra labor and equipment. "It's pretty tight once you get the environmental control units hooked up to it," Bias said. "And it uses positive air pressure to keep everything out."

Personal Information Carrier

U.S. military personnel used to wear metal dog tags with name, rank, serial number, and blood type. But now troops will wear the personal information carrier (PIC). This dog tag–sized device provides personnel with a small computer chip for storing personal medical data. The PIC has a storage capacity of up to 128 megabytes. With the PIC, treatment data can be captured in a deployment situation, regardless of the communications infrastructure or the patient's evacuation route.

According to Colonel John Holcomb, the army surgeon general's trauma consultant, "Paper goes thousands of miles and through dozens of hands, and it doesn't always make it. . . . In Operation Iraqi Freedom, I've seen doctors resort to writing notes on patients' dressings to let the

next care provider know what was done. My personal opinion is they need to wear their record on their neck."

A patient's medical records can be accessed and updated by medical personnel through a special adapter on a personal digital assistant or a laptop computer. By 2005, plans were in motion to develop an even more high-tech system, a wireless electronic information carrier.

A Stretcher-Sized Intensive Care Unit

Emergency room doctors are often heard shouting the word "Stat!" But now doctors in forward military hospital facilities will be heard shouting "LSTAT!"

During the last century, there were a few improvements in the technology of stretchers. There was the Stokes litter, a reinforced basket that protected the patient, but for the most part, stretchers were stretchers. Now the army has the life support for trauma and transport (LSTAT). This high-tech litter contains a ventilator, suction, oxygen system, infusion pump, physiological monitor, clinical blood analyzer, and defibrillator. More than a stretcher, it is an individualized portable intensive care system and surgical platform!

The LSTAT provides resuscitation and stabilization capability through an integrated set of state-of-the-art medical mechanisms. It was discovered in World War II that lives were saved exponentially in direct proportion to how close first-aid stations and field hospitals were to the front. In the late twentieth century, the Army Medical Corps continued to build on this practice.

During an August 2001 field evaluation, soldiers of the U.S. Army's Task Force Med Falcon move a patient at Camp Bondsteel in Kosovo, using the life support for trauma and transport (LSTAT). *Photo courtesy of Task Force Med Falcon*

The first Stryker MEVs were delivered to the Stryker Brigade Combat Team at Fort Lewis, Washington, in March 2003. Such vehicles are capable of moving at sustained speeds of up to sixty miles per hour, as fast as typical civilian ambulances. *U.S. Army Medical Department*

LSTAT is perhaps the ultimate means of moving trauma care farther forward toward the site of an injury, and the medical corps continues to improve diagnostics and therapeutics throughout the evacuation and treatment process.

Stryker MEV

The Stryker is a highly deployable wheeled armored vehicle that recently entered U.S. Army service. It is designed to combine the attributes of firepower, battlefield mobility, survivability, and versatility, with reduced maintenance and logistical requirements. The Stryker is a nineteen-ton, eight-wheeled vehicle that can sustain speeds of sixty miles per hour. It can be forward deployed by C-130 aircraft and be immediately combat-capable upon its arrival in any contingency area. The Stryker can be armed with a remote weapon station with a .50-caliber machine gun or Mk.19 40-mm grenade launcher. As an infantry carrier, it carries a nine-man infantry squad and a crew of two.

Formally named in February 2002, its dual namesakes were two army Medal of Honor recipients, Private First Class Stuart Stryker, who served in World War II, and Specialist Robert Stryker, who served in Vietnam. The Stryker family of vehicles includes the infantry carrier vehicle, mobile gun system, antitank guided-missile vehicle, mortar-carrier vehicle, reconnaissance vehicle, fire-support vehicle, engineer squad vehicle, commander's vehicle, and a nuclear, biological, and chemical recon-naissance vehicle.

By the end of 2002, plans were in motion for deploying a Stryker medical evacuation vehicle (MEV). According to Steve Reichard, the Army Medical Materiel Development Activity product manager, "The important thing is it [the MEV] has the mobility and ability to keep up with the forces. It lets us actually be there when we're needed. . . . In Desert Storm, we were routinely one to two hours behind the forces."

First delivered to the Stryker Brigade Combat Team at Fort Lewis, Washington, in March 2003, the Stryker MEV can evacuate four litter patients or six ambulatory patients while its crew of three medics provides basic medical care. The Stryker

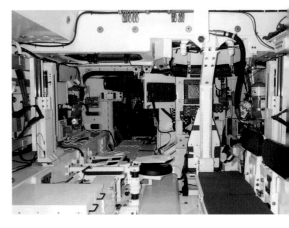

The interior of the Stryker medical evacuation vehicle includes a medical attendant's seat (center) that allows the attendant to view all patients and monitor all equipment simultaneously. It can evacuate four litter patients or six ambulatory patients while a crew of three medics provides basic medical care. The vehicle carries more medical supplies and equipment than older armored ambulances. *Project Managers Office, Brigade Combat Team*

MEV's interior also accommodates more medical supplies and equipment than the medevac variant of the M113 armored personnel carrier, and it has a higher ceiling, which provides a less cramped environment.

SIKA Combat Vehicle

The latest in surface combat vehicles, the SIKA provides stealthy all-weather reconnaissance and attack capability previously unavailable in ground vehicles. The stealth characteristics are derived from the vehicle's angular and non-reflective surfaces. SIKA incorporates many features described by its makers as "leap-ahead capabilities." These include an advanced sensor system capable of rapid wide-area searches, on-the-move operation, and long-range identification with an elevated mast. Live video images from the mast-mounted sensor system, known as Snake Eyes, are transmitted via satellite to commanders who are able to make quick, well-informed tactical decisions. The SIKA would carry a variety of types of armament similar to that of the M2 and M3 Bradley fighting vehicles. Such armament might include a 7.62mm machine gun and a TOW missile launcher, as well as a 25mm (or larger) cannon as a main gun.

The SIKA vehicle was developed by Lockheed Martin and others through an international collaborative program involving the United Kingdom's tactical reconnaissance armored combat equipment requirement (TRACER) and the United States' future scout and cavalry system (FSCS). These programs both specified a modern, survivable, state-of-the-art reconnaissance vehicle that could be deployed aboard a C-130 transport aircraft. The system's integration and packaging design enhances the sensor suite with a robust plug-and-play C4I (command, control, communications, computers, and intelligence) architecture. The SIKA vehicle was designed for a smooth ride over rough terrain and rapid, modular "pit-stop" maintenance for easy field repairs.

Snake Eyes

The Snake Eyes multi-spectral sensing system was designed to meet the initial requirements of the future combat systems envisioned for the U.S. Army's twenty-first century objective force. Incorporated into the SIKA combat vehicle, Snake Eyes provides reconnaissance, fire support, and targeting overmatch (meaning the system has more than enough capability to take on probable targets). Features include rapid wide-area searches, adverse-weather capability, and long-range target identification with an elevated mast. Designed to be easy to maintain in the field, Snake Eyes is a modular system in which built-in testing isolates faults to low-cost replaceable units, allowing for field replacement an estimated 95 percent of the time.

Multi-Band Multi-Mission Radio

In the twenty-first century, few components within the United States armed services have grown in importance more than special operations

The Snake Eyes elevated mast allows the SIKA combat vehicle to safely observe the enemy while masking itself from hostile fire. This demonstration was conducted at the U.S. Army's Fort Carson in Colorado in June 2002.
Lockheed Martin

The SIKA combat vehicle is seen here during field trials at the U.S. Army's Fort Carson in Colorado in June 2002. SIKA is a stealthy all-weather reconnaissance and attack vehicle.
Lockheed Martin

forces. The need to support commandos in remote locations is one of the key challenges, and one of the key aspects of this challenge is communications. To this end, the United States Special Operations Command (USSOCOM) issued a contract to Raytheon to produce the multi-band multi-mission (MBMMR) variation on its PSC-5D radio. The MBMMR-PSC-5 is an enhanced communication system that will be used by the special operations units of the army, navy, and air force. The initial order included 2 vehicular and 227 manpack systems to be produced at Raytheon C3I's manufacturing facility in Largo, Florida.

Technically, the MBMMR includes an enhanced key management system for state-of-the-art secure communications links and high-speed line-of-sight data transmission. Of great importance is the reduced weight of the new radio and the fact that it replaces several single-band radio systems currently used to communicate on different networks.

Water Buffalo

Important equipment for today's special operations forces is versatile secure communications equipment like the MBMMR-PSC-5 radio. Raytheon

Much of the hardware discussed in this chapter is decidedly high-tech. However, one vital system is about as basic as any that has served military personnel in any conflict. Napoleon said that an army travels on its stomach, and one commodity even more basic than food is water. When the U.S. military went to war in the Middle East, it found itself in a hot, dry environment.

Logistics experts worked hard to fulfill the needs of the thirsty soldiers, airmen, and marines. In Gulf War II, forty-five million 1.5-liter bottles were consumed each month at the height of the action. The water had been bottled in Turkey, Jordan, Saudi Arabia, and Greece. From there, it was shipped to Kuwait, where it was offloaded from ships and trucked throughout Iraq.

To augment bottled water, or to supply water in areas farther away from seaports, the U.S. Army's reverse osmosis water purification units (ROWPU) place purified water into the Water Buffalos, which are four-hundred-gallon steel tanks mounted on trailers. The technology may be centuries old, but the water is pure, and it gets to the thirsty soldiers when they need it.

NightSight

Using uncooled thermal-imaging technology, the Raytheon NightSight system is an improvement over conventional image-intensifier night-vision systems in that it operates in total darkness. Conversely, it will not shut down or "bloom" in sudden bright-light conditions that are often encountered on the battlefield. In addition, it allows its user to see through smoke and haze, and it is applicable to air and sea, as well as land, operations. It has the clarity to distinguish a human being at a distance of about half a mile.

U.S. Army preventive medicine personnel inspect a Water Buffalo at a forward operating location in Uzbekistan. The Buffalo is a mobile trailer used to store and transport safe drinking water to deployed soldiers. *Photo by Ben Bunger, U.S. Army Center for Health Promotion and Preventive Medicine*

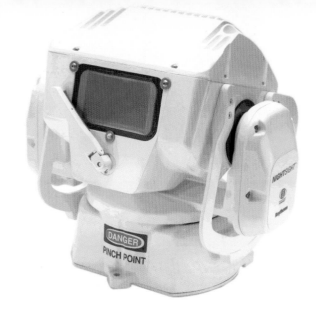

The NightSight drivers vision enhancer (DVE) for weapons and armored vehicles was designed so that its sensor and display control module were usable in any wheeled or tracked vehicle equipped with an interface adapter, and it runs off vehicle power. It is also designed to be light, rugged, and easy to use under the most trying of conditions.

The NightSight 200 Series unit for fixed locations incorporates a swiveling mechanism, and there are lens wiper–equipped and waterproof marine versions. It has a standard video interface and is VCR compatible.

Technically, NightSight operates in the far infrared spectrum, sensing the temperature differences between objects. Warmer objects will appear either darker or lighter, depending upon how the operator chooses to set the sight.

Handheld Thermal Imager

Members of the NightSight family of thermal imaging hardware are the Raytheon Palm IR series of cameras. These include the Palm IR 225 compact thermal imager and the IR 250D, an upgrade of the older IR 250 that is marketed in the same price range as older analog systems. The Palm IR 400D is a high-resolution (320x240)

color thermal-imaging system based on Raytheon's exclusive Digital Barium Strontium Titanate (BST) detector technology. The Palm IR 500 is the first radiometric camera from Raytheon that is based on their exclusive BST detector technology.

Javelin

The twenty-first-century successor to a long line of shoulder-fired weapons dating back to the bazooka of World War II, the FGM-148 Javelin is considered to be the world's premier shoulder-fired anti-armor weapon. The weapon was developed and produced for the U.S. Army by a joint venture between Lockheed Martin in Orlando, Florida, and Raytheon in Lewisville, Texas. A successor to the earlier Dragon shoulder-launched

The NightSight 200 thermal imager can detect objects the size of people a half mile away on moonless nights. *Raytheon*

The Palm IR Pro handheld thermal imager incorporates digital BST detector technology for nighttime imaging. *Raytheon*

The NightSight driver's vision enhancer (DVE) provides the operators of nearly every vehicle in the U.S. Army with the ability to see in total darkness. *Raytheon*

To fire the Javelin, the gunner places a cursor over the selected target. The command launch unit then sends a lock-on-before-launch signal to the missile. With its soft-launch design, the Javelin can be safely fired from *inside* buildings or bunkers. *Lockheed Martin*

weapon, the Javelin began equipping operational units just before the turn of the century.

The Javelin includes an imaging infrared missile and a command launch unit consisting of a day sight for use in clear conditions, as well as an imaging infrared sight for use at night and in reduced visibility. Using an arched top-attack profile, Javelin climbs above its target for improved visibility and then strikes where the armor is weakest. A fire-and-forget system, Javelin automatically guides itself to the target after launch, allowing the gunner time to take cover and avoid enemy fire. Soldiers or marines can reposition immediately after firing, or reload to engage another threat.

Idaho Integrated Breaching Shotgun

The problem presented to the engineers at the Idaho National Engineering and Environmental Laboratory (INEEL) was to create a better firearm for use in executing forced entries through doors. Traditionally, a shotgun is used to destroy the hinges or locks, then the shooter switches from the shotgun to an assault rifle or waits for others to precede him through the door. This second step costs valuable seconds in the process.

The result of INEEL's efforts is the integrated breaching shotgun, a combination shotgun and assault weapon. It was designed by engineer Steve Frickey, along with David Crandall and Rich Watson from the National Security

Special Programs Group, and Mike Occhionero of INEEL.

The process involved redesigning the traditional twelve-gauge pump shotgun. Standard shotguns cycle cartridges by moving the bolt to the rear. In the new design, the bolt is held stationary and the receiver and barrel move forward, allowing the receiver to be shortened and the barrel to be lengthened. Making the barrel longer provides more time for the powder to burn and more energy to be applied to the projectile, making the shotgun more effective. The new weapon also incorporates a replaceable box magazine, making it easier to rapidly reload and select alternate munitions, such as less-than-lethal rounds.

As Occhionero pointed out, "Typically, a gun design program is a multi-year, multimillion-dollar proposition." However, by using existing components in an innovative way, the team was able to design the prototype in little more than two months.

The Mule

During the conflicts of the early twenty-first century, as the U.S. Air Force was embracing robotic technology for a successful and highly publicized roster of unmanned aerial vehicles (UAVs), the U.S. Army was looking at robotic technology for ground warfare. Under the general umbrella of its future combat systems program, the army has embraced the multifunction utility-logistics and equipment (MULE) vehicle. It is a system cleverly

The integrated breaching shotgun was developed by Idaho National Engineering and Environmental Laboratory engineers to be used in breaking down doors. It combines a shotgun and a rifle into a single weapon. *INEEL*

named with an acronym that refers back a century or more to an era when the four-legged, oat-eating army mule was the ubiquitous form of logistical transport for this branch of the armed forces.

The twenty-first-century MULE was created by Lockheed Martin to move forward into system development and demonstration (SDD) and ultimately into production. The MULE was envisioned as uniquely supporting the U.S. Army's transformation to a lighter and more mobile fighting force.

As with the UAVs, the air force says the MULE will undertake the dull, dirty, and dangerous jobs of the current forces. In other words, long, dull, repetitive reconnaissance missions; missions into a battlefield environment made dirty by chemical or biological weapons; or missions against targets that are very dangerous for humans. As with UAVs, the MULE is envisioned as increasing the efficiency of the total force by complementing, not replacing, human soldiers and manned-platform functions.

The MULE is a large vehicle in the 2.5-ton weight class. It operates on an advanced 6x6 independent articulated suspension, coupled with in-hub motors powering each wheel. This provides extreme mobility in complex terrain, far exceeding that of vehicles utilizing more conventional suspension systems. It is said that the

MULE would be able to go everywhere a soldier can go and more. It will climb a nearly vertical five-foot incline, far exceeding requirements.

In most terrain, the twenty-first-century MULE, like the mule of old, will be sufficiently surefooted to safely follow dismounted troops over rough terrain, through rock and debris fields, and over urban rubble. It will cross five-foot gaps, climb over twenty-inch obstacles, negotiate side slopes greater than 40 percent, and ford water that is four feet deep, overpass obstacles as high as a half meter, while compensating for varying payload weights and center of gravity locations.

Initially, three variations on the MULE were envisioned. First, there is the transport MULE, with the volume and payload capacity to carry the equipment and supplies to support two dismounted infantry squads. It is also capable of being used for casualty evacuation. Next is the attack MULE, formally designated as the armed robotic vehicle, assault (light), or ARV-A (L). It will be armed with a rapid-fire suppressive weapon, such as a heavy machine gun, and will have antitank capability. It is designed to provide immediate, heavy firepower to the infantry soldier. Finally, the countermine MULE is designed to provide detection and marking of land mines and minefields.

The army's MULE, the multifunction utility-logistics and equipment vehicle, comes in the three variants seen here: a transport, a light assault vehicle, and a system for detecting and neutralizing land mines. *Lockheed Martin*

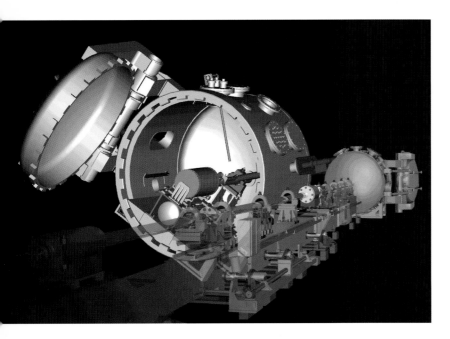

The JASPER (joint actinide shock physics experimental research) gas gun is a two-stage system first tested in 2003 at the Nevada Test Site. *Lawrence Livermore National Laboratory*

One only hopes that the MULE won't be as stubborn as its four-legged predecessor.

JASPER Gas Gun

Since the darkest days of the Cold War, leading-edge, stranger-than-fiction weapons systems have typically passed through their experimental phase at the Nevada Test Range, formerly managed by the Atomic Energy Commission (AEC), and now managed by the Department of Energy (DOE). It was under the AEC that this enormous test range was divided into numbered "areas." Everyone has heard of Area 51, one of the sectors of this range.

In the twenty-first century, such a system tested there has been the JASPER (joint actinide shock physics experimental research), a one-hundred-foot two-stage gas gun, which was designed at the Lawrence Livermore National Laboratory near San Francisco. Despite the implications of the term "gas gun," JASPER is not a weapon itself, but a mechanism to ensure the safety and reliability of the United States nuclear arsenal. To meet this challenge, scientists need better data showing how plutonium, a key component of nuclear warheads, behaves under extreme pressures and temperatures. As the DOE points out, a well-established experimental technique for determining the properties of materials at high pressures, temperatures, and strain rates is to use a gas gun to shock a small sample of material with a projectile traveling at

high velocity and then diagnose the material's response. Lawrence Livermore's two-stage gas guns have made important contributions to such studies. For example, in 1996, what was then Livermore's largest gas gun produced metallic hydrogen for the first time.

On July 8, 2003, in its first test, JASPER fired a projectile weighing one ounce, which impacted a slightly heavier plutonium target at a speed of about 3.2 miles per second. Considered an unqualified success, this experiment marked the culmination of years of effort. As Lawrence Livermore had observed, ongoing experiments have drawn enthusiastic praise from throughout the DOE, the National Nuclear Security Administration (NNSA), and the scientific community.

Sniper XR

According to William Scott, writing in the October 4, 2004, issue of *Aviation Week*, the U.S. Air Force's Sniper XR advanced-targeting pod "allows pilots to put a single bomb through a window from long standoff ranges." Indeed, the XR in the name stands for extended range.

Sniper XR's outstanding precision performance is said to be the result of a superior optical design combined with advanced image-processing algorithms. Demonstrating exceptional stability and pointing accuracy in U.S. Air Force flight tests, the pod performed well throughout the entire F-16 flight envelope, including supersonic flight.

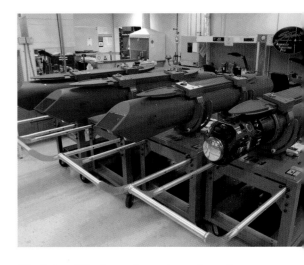

The Sniper XR advanced targeting pod was first delivered to equip the U.S. Air Force's F-16CJ Block 50 aircraft, but was designed for several current and future fighter aircraft. *Lockheed Martin*

The Sniper XR advanced targeting pod incorporates high-resolution FLIR, as well as a dual-mode laser, a CCD television camera, a laser spot tracker, and a laser marker. *Lockheed Martin*

Developed by Lockheed Martin's Missiles and Fire Control group, Sniper is a precision targeting system in a single, lightweight pod that incorporates a dual-mode laser, a CCD-television, and high-resolution, mid-wave third-generation forward-looking infrared (FLIR). With a laser spot tracker and a laser marker, the Sniper XR greatly improves target detection and identification. Designed to be compatible with current standoff weaponry, the pod provides automatic tracking and laser designation of tactical-size targets via real-time imagery presented on cockpit displays. Likewise, the supersonic, low-observable design results in a substantial reduction in drag and weight.

Sniper is a cousin to the earlier AN/AAS-38B Nite Hawk targeting system and uses the same aircraft interfaces. Nite Hawk was designed to identify, automatically track, and laser-designate tactical targets for pilots of the U.S. Navy or Marine Corps F/A-18 Hornet and Super Hornet aircraft.

The Sniper XR pods initially equipped the U.S. Air Force's F-16CJ Block 50 aircraft and the Air National Guard's F-16 Block 30 aircraft. The U.S. Air Force plans to buy as many as 522 Sniper pods for use on A-10 and F-15E Strike Eagle aircraft as well as F-16s. The system is in service with the Royal Norwegian Air Force under the name Pantera.

TADS/PNVS

They call it "the eyes of the Apache," and by night, that is essentially true. The Lockheed Martin target acquisition designation sight/pilot night-vision sensor (TADS/PNVS) is a twenty-first-century high-tech system that enables pilots of the U.S. Army's AH-64 Apache attack helicopters to fly at very low altitudes in total darkness and in poor weather. It allows them to see ground targets under these conditions and to destroy them at standoff ranges.

The TADS/PNVS consists of two subsystems that can be installed and operated independently.

Seen in the nose of this AH-64D Apache attack chopper, the rotating turret contains the TADS/PNVS infrared sensor system for target detection during night operations. These sensors are linked to cockpit displays and helmet-mounted controls that magnify the expanse of terrain in the pilot's line of sight—and they can be directed manually or controlled by the head movements of a crewmember. *Lockheed Martin*

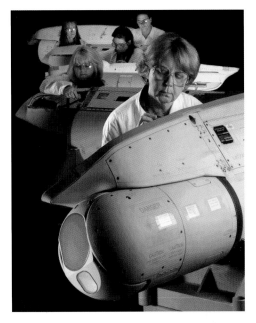

Skilled technicians at work on Nite Hawk targeting pods for F/A-18 aircraft. Nite Hawk was a precursor to Sniper. *Lockheed Martin*

Housed in a rotating turret mounted on the nose of the Apache is an infrared sensor for target detection during night flights. The direct-view optics (which consist of a high-powered telescope and a television camera, a laser spot tracker, and laser-designator rangefinder) pinpoint targets for laser-guided weapons such as the AGM-114 Hellfire missile. By 2004, TADS/PNVS equipped fourteen active-duty U.S. Army units and eleven National Guard and Army Reserve units.

Arrowhead

The U.S. Army's modernized target acquisition designation sight/pilot night vision sensor (M-TADS/PNVS) system is trademarked by Lockheed Martin as Arrowhead. The system's modular architecture accommodates a field-retrofit from earlier-generation TADS/PNVS to the new Arrowhead configuration on both AH-64A and AH-64D Apache attack helicopters.

Initially flight-tested in 1999, Arrowhead became the current state of the art in an advanced electro-optical fire-control system that Apache pilots can use for safe flight by day, night, or in bad-weather missions. Compared to the previous systems, the Arrowhead's advanced technology improves system performance by more than 150 percent. Reliability is said to have increased by more than 150 percent as well, while maintenance actions have decreased approximately 60 percent. Meanwhile, streamlining field maintenance by concentrating parts and

The lightweight Arrowhead modules can be rapidly removed and replaced by AH-64 Apache crews in the field and on the flightline. *Lockheed Martin*

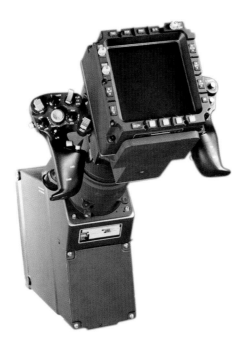

In both the AH-64A and AH-64D, the TEDAC provides an enhanced crewstation interface to the modernized target acquisition and designation sight, better known as Arrowhead. TEDAC replaces the old optical relay tube. *Lockheed Martin*

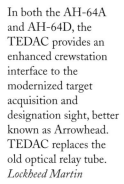

TEDAC presents the copilot-gunner in the Apache attack helicopter with sensor video on a high-resolution active-matrix liquid-crystal display and provides sensor controls through a modernized bezel and left and right handgrips. *Lockheed Martin*

tools in fewer types of depots saves time and operational costs over the life of the system.

TEDAC

TEDAC, the abbreviation for target acquisition designation sight (TADS) electronics display and control assembly, is the modernized replacement for the old twentieth-century optical relay tube located in the crewstation of the co-pilot/gunner aboard the U.S. Army's AH-64 Apache attack helicopter. The system replaces the optical relay tube's small cathode-ray-tube display and direct-view optics with a large ten-inch-square flat-panel cockpit display that gives the gunner high-resolution sensor video from the Arrowhead.

TEDAC utilizes an active-matrix liquid-crystal display. This theoretically improves the

The Hawkeye XR TSS, seen in the nose of this AH-1 Cobra attack helicopter, offers precision target tracking and laser designation up to and beyond the maximum range of the Hellfire missiles the copter carries. *Lockheed Martin*

gunner's ability to engage targets, while providing greater situational awareness and more space in the cockpit. The modular design and improved fault detection allow for simpler maintenance and support.

Hawkeye

Hawkeye is the nickname for the extended-range-target sight system (XR TSS), a multi-sensor electro-optical infrared fire-control system. For more than three decades in the twentieth century, the Bell AH-1 Cobra gave the U.S. Marine Corps potent and capable attack-helicopter capability. In the twenty-first century, Hawkeye was developed to give the Cobra, specifically the AH-1Z, a state-of-the-art targeting system utilizing a third-generation forward-looking infrared (FLIR) system. Originally developed for the AH-1Z, Hawkeye is also available for integration on the AH-1F and AH-1S, as well as other choppers and fixed-wing aircraft.

Technically, Hawkeye includes a large-aperture mid-wave FLIR, color television, laser designator and rangefinder (with eyesafe mode), laser spot tracker, and on-gimbal inertial measurement unit. Hawkeye gives Cobra drivers the ability to identify and laze (laser designate) targets at the maximum range of an AGM-114 Hellfire. This significantly enhances both survivability and lethality.

MCR/CHAOS

Since it was founded in September 1952 by E. O. Lawrence and Edward Teller, the work of the Lawrence Livermore National Laboratory near San Francisco has included the development and testing of nuclear weapons and other high-tech weapons systems. In order to execute its work, Lawrence Livermore has depended on leading-edge computing technology. When Lawrence and Teller took delivery of their first supercomputer in 1953, it was the Remington-Rand UNIVAC-1, a massive monster with more than 5,600 vacuum tubes and memory that could store nine kilobytes of data—hardly impressive by modern standards, but pretty amazing in its day.

Through the years, the laboratory's computing power has kept pace with leading-edge standards. Lawrence Livermore is still playing a key role in realistic simulations under the Department of Energy's National Nuclear Security Administration (NNSA) program to ensure the safety and

reliability of the nation's weapons stockpile, with the multiprogrammatic capability resource (MCR) supercomputer coming online. It is a 11.2-teraflop tightly coupled Linux cluster, containing 1,152 nodes, each with two 2.4-GHz Pentium 4 Xenon processors and four gigabytes of memory.

MCR runs the Lawrence Livermore CHAOS (clustered high-availability operating system) software, which incorporates the Red Hat Linux operating system. The Livermore Computing Linux clusters, which provide the Livermore model programming environment to laboratory scientists, share a common cluster architecture and use similar hardware components where possible. CHAOS is derived from a Red Hat "boxed set" release, and is resynchronized at each Red Hat minor release, approximately every six months. By tracking Red Hat releases, CHAOS benefits from Red Hat's integration testing and feedback from a large desktop computing user base.

Project Grasp

As noted previously, the general fascination with flying saucers has been part of popular culture since the term was coined in 1947. Meanwhile, the fascination with the technology that popular mythology attributes to them has intrigued aeronautical engineers, especially within the military, for at least as long.

Leaving the extraterrestrial explanation of flying saucers for Hollywood to exploit, one is left to ponder whether or not aeronautics might ever be able to exploit a scientific principal in which a circular electromagnetic device might create lift. For half a century, the answer was a firm "probably

The huge multiprogrammatic capability resource computer runs the CHAOS software environment, which incorporates the Red Hat Linux operating system. *Lawrence Livermore National Laboratory*

not." Then, in July 2002, the BBC reported that the controversial Russian scientist Yevgeny Podkletnov was trying to "create a device that will defy gravity."

Such a news item would hardly have been worth repeating had the BBC not also said that Podkletnov's work was being taken seriously by the world's largest aircraft maker, Boeing. The BBC went on to say that George Muellner, head of the Phantom Works—the advanced R&D unit for Boeing—had told the security analysis journal *Jane's Defence Weekly* that the science appeared to be valid and plausible. The BBC reported erroneously that "the hypothesis is being tested [by Boeing] in a program code-named Project Grasp."

In a response to the BBC news item, Boeing commented that:

> Phantom Works is always monitoring potentially breakthrough ideas and technologies. We are aware of Podkletnov's work on "anti-gravity" devices and would be interested in seeing further development work being done. However, Boeing is not funding any activities in this area at this time. The recent report that we are is based on a misinterpretation of information. For instance, GRASP is not a code name for a current project but rather an acronym for a presentation entitled "Gravity Research for Advanced Space Propulsion," in which a Boeing engineer explains Podkletnov's theory and proposes that we should continue to monitor this work and perhaps even conduct some low-cost experiments to further assess its plausibility. No steps have been taken beyond this point by Boeing.

Podkletnov claimed to have countered the effects of gravity in an experiment at the Tampere University of Technology in Finland in 1992. He explained that he found that objects above a superconducting ceramic disc rotating over powerful electromagnets lost approximately 2 percent of their weight. The BBC reported that NASA had attempted to reproduce Podkletnov's experiment, but that a preliminary report had indicated that tests "gave a null result."

The XM30 guided multiple-launch rocket system offers the potential of one round, one kill capability. *Lockheed Martin*

XM30

It can be said that the XM30 is a virtual poster child for twenty-first-century guided munitions, as it embodies a "one round, one kill" capability. Such low-cost, low-risk munitions are characteristic of weapons developed against a backdrop of a growing abhorrence of collateral damage. To achieve this desired—and certainly desirable—objective, the Lockheed Martin XM30 is equipped with an enhanced anti-jam and accuracy processor.

Known as the guided multiple launch rocket system (GMLRS), the XM30 is actually part of the MLRS family of munitions that includes three types of rockets and four missiles, with an additional six variants in development. GMLRS boasts an inertial guidance package that is aided by a global positioning system and integrated in a rocket body. Small canards on the guided rocket nose will add basic maneuverability to further enhance the accuracy of the system. The modular design facilitates future growth within the family, which is part of an international cooperative program involving the United Kingdom, Italy, France, and Germany, as well as the U.S. Army. Technically, the MLRS carries a warhead with a payload consisting of more than four hundred submunitions, or bomblets, that can be delivered over a range in excess of thirty-seven miles. The XM30 integrates a two-hundred-pound unitary warhead into the system. It has a range of up to forty miles, with accuracy measured in a few yards. The warhead contains a payload of 404 dual-purpose improved conventional munitions (DPICM) bomblets.

XM982 Excalibur

Like the XM30, the XM982 is a current one round, one kill guided munition. Developed jointly by Raytheon and Bofors Defense, the Excalibur is a smart artillery round. Fired from a conventional 155-mm howitzer, the XM982 has a range of twenty-five miles. It is fired for high elevation and then glides to the target like any shell, except that it can maneuver itself for a perfect hit using the global positioning system (GPS) and an inertial navigation system (INS) guidance device to control four canard fins. The payload can include a single unitary warhead or multiple submunitions.

In October 2004, Tyco Electronics received an initial development contract from Raytheon Missiles Systems for the tactical telemetry module and antennas for the XM982. The tactical telemetry module contains signal conditioning, data encoding, a high-efficiency S-Band transmitter, and power-control functions. It will telemeter critical onboard sensor and system information during the projectile's flight. The practical benefits of this telemetry feature include midcourse retargeting and trajectory fine tuning.

The Excalibur XM982 is a family of 155mm smart artillery rounds that use rotating fins for roll stabilization. In actual combat, the projectiles would not carry inert payloads. *Raytheon*

The XM982 projectile is designed to contain eighty-five dual-purpose XM80 submunitions.

EX-171

As a major component of the U.S. Navy's twenty-first-century Sea Power 21 Sea Strike concept, Raytheon developed the EX-171 extended-range guided munition (ERGM). This new projectile combines increased range with GPS and an inertial navigation guidance system to support U.S. Marine Corps forces ashore with sustained and accurate fire from naval vessels. The ERGM is designed to be used by existing five-inch guns, and also in the U.S. Navy's next generation DD(X) advanced gun system.

LOSAT

When land warfare types speak of anti-armor weapons and the phrase "tremendous overmatch lethality" comes up, it is often in the same sentence with mention of the Lockheed Martin line-of-sight antitank (LOSAT) system. The system was created to give rapid-reaction forced-entry/early-entry forces decisive lethality against heavy armor. This weapon uses a second-generation forward-looking infrared (FLIR)/video acquisition sensor, which is mounted on a heavy air-mobile Humvee chassis, but on the business end are LOSAT's kinetic energy missiles (KEM). They are casually described as being capable of defeating all predicted future armored combat vehicles.

Each kinetic energy missile weighs 174 pounds, is 113 inches long and 6.4 inches in diameter. The LOSAT travels at a speed of five

A dramatic artist's rendering shows an EX-171 extended-range guided munition (ERGM) being fired from a five-inch gun on a U.S. Navy destroyer at sea. *Raytheon*

The mobile and extremely lethal line-of-sight antitank (LOSAT) weapon system is said to be capable of defeating all predicted future armored combat vehicles, not to mention making fast work of fortified bunkers. *Lockheed Martin*

thousand feet per second, meaning that it reaches its maximum range in less than five seconds. Being a kinetic energy weapon, it has no explosive warhead. But it carries a long penetrator that destroys the target by the force of the impact, like a medieval spear traveling at unimaginable speed. The system is extremely mobile, and the superior cross-country mobility of the Humvee is not compromised by the addition of the LOSAT system. Indeed, the LOSAT-equipped Humvee can be moved across the battlefield by sling load with a UH-60L Blackhawk helicopter. The LOSAT is designed for a three-man crew, but a crew of two can also conduct engagements. The system can be reloaded in less than ten minutes using onboard material handling equipment.

Compact Kinetic Energy Missile

As the name implies, the compact kinetic energy missile (CKEM) is a hit-to-kill weapon that uses extremely high velocity and kinetic energy, rather than an explosive charge, to destroy its target. The targets would include enemy vehicles with explosive reactive armor that is designed to explode on contact, destroying high-explosive warheads before they penetrate the vehicle. The high velocity would be speeds in excess of 6.5 times the speed of sound.

An evolution of the LOSAT program, CKEM is a hypervelocity antitank projectile developed by the Army Aviation and Missile Command (AMCOM) under the overarching umbrella of the U.S. Army future combat systems program. In

An artist's conception of a compact kinetic energy missile (CKEM) being launched from a U.S. Army future combat vehicle (FCV). *Lockheed Martin*

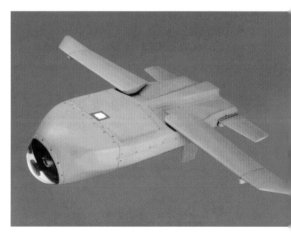

The five-foot, one-hundred-pound compact kinetic energy missile (CKEM), seen here in flight, is a hypervelocity antitank round designed to be launched from both ground platforms and helicopters. *Lockheed Martin*

June 2004, the army selected Lockheed Martin to produce the projectile. The idea is that it would be used to arm heavy ground platforms and attack helicopters, as well as the army's future combat vehicle (FCV). The CKEM would have an internal guidance mechanism that would permit the launching vehicle to fire while on the move.

LOCAAS

The future of precision-guided munitions in the twenty-first century is embodied in the characteristics of the low-cost autonomous attack system (LOCAAS) smart submunition that is being developed by Lockheed Martin Missiles & Fire Control for the U.S. Air Force and U.S. Army. LOCAAS is

The low-cost autonomous attack system (LOCAAS) attacks in swarms, ignores targets other than its own, and is able to loiter over a target area for extended periods while waiting to strike. Note the folding wing feature. *Lockheed Martin*

just thirty inches long, with a wingspan of forty inches. It is capable of broad area search, identification, and destruction of mobile ground targets. The LOCAAS is designed to operate without internal propulsion, but there is a powered version, the P-LOCAAS, equipped with a small turbojet engine. This variant is capable of loitering above its target for about a half-hour before striking. Both the powered LOCAAS and the unpowered LOCAAS can be dispensed from the air force SU-64 tactical munition dispenser, an internal weapons bay carriage, a munition ejector rack, or external pylons. Both can also be dispensed from the U.S. Army's multiple launch rocket system (MLRS) rocket.

Each type also carries a multimode penetrator warhead. Multimode means that once the target is found, LOCAAS would release a metal warhead that could be shaped as a penetrating rod, a slug, or a cloud of shrapnel. Target aimpoint and warhead mode are automatically determined by the laser radar (LADAR) seeker.

ATACMS and BAT

The army tactical missile system (ATACMS) is a family of missiles that have been operational since Gulf War I, when thirty-two missiles were successfully fired, and it's likely to be of particular note for some time to come. The ATACMS Block I missiles, of which more than 1,600 were

The ATACMS universal dispenser is a modular and flexible system designed for the integration of a variety of differing-size munitions into the system's Block II missile. The structure and dispenser subsystems are identical for a range of munition options. *Lockheed Martin*

produced and fielded, fire 950 M74 antipersonnel submunitions at ranges up to one hundred miles. The Block IA had a reduced payload of three hundred M74 submunitions, but a maximum range of nearly two hundred miles, and an improved guidance package using the global positioning system.

The ATACMS Block II solid-fuel missile carries thirteen brilliant anti-armor (BAT) submunitions. The BAT was produced by Northrop Grumman, with Raytheon Company as the principal subcontractor responsible for BAT's infrared elements. Production continued through 2003. These submunitions are dispensed by a gas-bag management system and provide a deep-attack capability against moving targets at a range of ninety miles. The BAT uses passive acoustic and infrared sensors to find, attack, and destroy moving vehicles deep in enemy territory.

HIMARS

A member of the U.S. Army's multiple launch rocket system (MLRS) family of munitions, the high-mobility artillery rocket system (HIMARS) is designed to place overwhelming fire support at the disposal of light, quickly deployed forces. It puts MLRS firepower on wheels, and these wheels can be moved rapidly into areas previously inaccessible to heavy weapons of this type. The wheeled chassis is a five-ton, 6x6 truck developed by the army as part of its family of medium tactical vehicles (FMTV) program. The

The BAT submunition can operate effectively day or night and in adverse weather conditions. It is an unpowered, aerodynamically stable glider 36 inches long, 5.5 inches in diameter with its wings folded, and forty-four pounds in weight. *Raytheon*

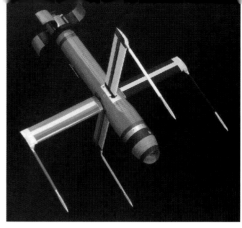

Viper Strike, a derivative of the BAT submunition, looks more like a praying mantis than a viper or a bat. *Northrop Grumman*

This stunning composite photo depicts a salvo launch of multiple high-mobility artillery rocket system (HIMARS) weapons. HIMARS carries a single six-pack of rockets on the U.S. Army's five-ton truck. *Lockheed Martin*

truck can be transported by a C-130 airlifter and can carry a single six-pack of HIMARS rockets or one army tactical missile system (ATACMS) weapon.

Built by Lockheed Martin, HIMARS was first successfully deployed by the army's XVIII Airborne Corps, and in 2000, the U.S. Marine Corps joined the program. HIMARS is ideal for rapid deployment with either the marines or the army airborne units. Each HIMARS truck is operated by a crew of three, a driver, a gunner and the section chief, although the fire-control system is such that even a single soldier can fire it, and firing can be in automatic or manual mode.

Viper Strike

Developed at Northrop Grumman's Land Combat Systems facility at Redstone Arsenal in Huntsville, Alabama, Viper Strike is a derivative of the brilliant anti-armor (BAT) submunition previously produced by Northrop Grumman and Raytheon. Viper Strike is designed for air-to-ground operations that require a steep angle of attack, particularly in mountainous terrain and urban areas where strict rules of engagement are operative. It uses a semi-active laser seeker to home in on a target that has been designated, or lazed, by a soldier on the ground. The idea is to achieve the greatest possible accuracy while minimizing collateral damage.

Viper Strike has a warhead that is smaller than that of the AGM-114 Hellfire used by attack helicopters and by the U.S. Air Force MQ-1 Predator

drones. Typically, it carries a four-pound high-explosive anti-tank (HEAT) charge that has a self-destruct mechanism to eliminate hazards from unexploded (dud) munitions. Optional warhead configurations include blast fragmentation and thermobaric charges. (Thermobaric weapons, better known as fuel-air explosives, use atmospheric oxygen, rather than a chemical oxidizer.)

AGM-114K Hellfire II

Since the early 1980s, the AGM-114 Hellfire family of air-to-ground missiles has been widely used by the various branches of the United States armed services and by numerous allied countries. They have been used to equip aircraft

Not just for helicopters anymore, the AGM-114K Hellfire II is available for use on launch platforms such as this fast patrol boat. Platforms use acquisition and designation systems to effectively launch a Hellfire II missile for a precision kill. *Lockheed Martin*

This dramatic studio image of the AGM-158 joint air-to-surface standoff missile (JASSM) sends chills down the spine of the viewer. *Lockheed Martin*

from attack helicopters to MQ-1 Predator unmanned aerial vehicles. Indeed, more than thirty thousand examples of the basic AGM-114A have been delivered. The Hellfire's small size—less than six feet long with a weight of about one hundred pounds—has made it both versatile and flexible.

At the beginning of the twenty-first century, the AGM-114K Hellfire II modular missile system broadens the scope of both capabilities and launch platforms. Multiple warheads and guidance systems enable a great deal of customization. The Hellfire II family includes anti-armor and anti-shipping warhead configurations. Among these are the semi-active laser with an antitank high explosive and a blast-fragmentation warhead. It achieves pinpoint accuracy by homing in on reflected laser energy aimed at the target from the launching helicopter or ground-based observer. The AGM-114K now arms the U.S. Army's AH-64 Apache and the Marine Corps' AH-1 Super Cobra attack helicopters, as well as other platforms.

JASSM

The AGM-158 joint air-to-surface standoff missile (JASSM) is a long-range precision air-to-surface missile designed for the U.S. Air Force and U.S. Navy to use against high-value, well-defended targets. Its long range keeps aircrews well out of danger from hostile air-defense systems. After launch, it is able to fly autonomously over a circuitous low-level route to the area of a target, where an autonomous terminal guidance system will guide the missile in for a direct hit. As contractor Lockheed Martin points out, "With this superior performance and affordable price, JASSM offers the best value of any weapon in its class."

Initially, the AGM-158 was acquired for use on air force F-16s and B-52s, as well as the navy's F/A-18E and F/A-18F Super Hornets, but it is also compatible with a host of other aircraft, including the air force F-15E, F-117, B-1B and B-2, and the navy's shore-based P-3C and carrier-based S-3B. The air force alone plans to acquire more than four thousand JASSMs and extended-range JASSM-ERs.

RadScout

Extremely valuable, if not vital, in today's world is gear like the highly portable RadScout detector and analyzer. The RadScout is a handheld system for measuring energy released from radioactive material that will determine the specific material that produced the energy. It locates nuclear materials using a special germanium crystal to detect minute amounts of gamma rays and neutrons that all radioactive materials emit.

Developed within the Department of Energy's National Nuclear Security Administration's Lawrence Livermore National Laboratory nuclear

The handheld RadScout detector and analyzer measures energy released from radioactive material and then determines the specific material that produced the energy. It was developed by the Lawrence Livermore National Laboratory nuclear weapons program. *Lawrence Livermore National Laboratory*

weapons program, RadScout was created for military personnel, emergency first responders, and inspection personnel. In short, it's for anyone who needs rapid detection and identification of radioactive material to determine the nature and scope of a threat. RadScout measures neutrons and gamma rays emitted by radioactive materials, then analyzes them to identify the sources. Weighing about twenty pounds, RadScout features a miniaturized refrigeration system cooling to –280 degrees Fahrenheit that eliminates the need for the liquid nitrogen cooling systems traditionally used with germanium radiation detectors (liquid nitrogen being difficult to use in the field).

In 2002, Lawrence Livermore National Laboratory signed a licensing agreement with ORTEC Products, a business unit of AMETEK Incorporated, to commercialize the RadScout by incorporating the technology in the next generation of advanced portable nuclear detection systems.

Pulsed Photonuclear Neutron Detector

As noted in the previous entry, portable radiation detection equipment for field deployment is a key mandate within the National Nuclear Security Administration of the Department of Energy (DOE). Against this backdrop, there are a number of projects ongoing at the various DOE laboratories.

One such system is a pulsed photonuclear neutron detector that was developed at the Idaho National Engineering and Environmental Laboratory. It uses a transportable electron accelerator to produce energetic photons, which interact with a suspect object, such as a cargo container used in tests at the Idaho Accelerator Center in

Pocatello, Idaho. This process induces fission—divisions in the atomic nucleus—in nuclear material, and creates no reaction in other materials.

Physicist James Jones has designed a patent-pending cylindrical detector device that can pick up and identify such a fission occurrence. This pulsed photonuclear neutron detector senses the presence of shielded nuclear material and can differentiate between highly enriched uranium, depleted uranium, or thorium when a second beam at a different energy level is directed at the object.

CHARC

When it is possible to name a weapons system in such a way as to identify it with a compelling acronym, this is always desirable. Certainly this is the case with the covert high-speed attack and reconnaissance craft, whose acronym, CHARC, is pronounced "Shark." The CHARC is an amazing maritime craft that is said to take the offensive capabilities from an attack helicopter and provide them on a high-speed surface platform. Designed to protect large navy vessels from small, armed speedboats and submarines, CHARC is an amalgam of many advanced technologies that have been developed by Lockheed Martin.

CHARC is also designed to operate in the littoral environment, the areas near coastlines and intercoastal waterways. To accomplish such missions, the CHARC is semi-submersible, presenting a low radar and visual signature. It is geometrically reconfigurable, making it tall enough to withstand high seas, yet foldable so it can oper-

Physicist James Jones of the Idaho National Engineering and Environmental Laboratory is seen here at the Idaho Accelerator Center in Pocatello. He aims the accelerator beam of his pulsed photonuclear neutron detector at a huge mockup of a commercial cargo container sitting on the floor, and in less than two minutes it reveals the presence of uranium. *INEEL*

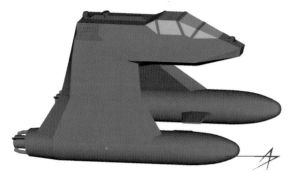

Few people fail to do a double take when they see the CHARC vehicle for the first time. Pronounced "shark," CHARC defies all preconceptions of what a small fast-attack vessel should look like. *Lockheed Martin*

ate in very shallow waters. Being foldable allows it to be easily taken aboard mother ships.

HALO Network

Orbiting high above an urban area, at an altitude higher than commercial airline traffic, an unmanned aerial vehicle (UAV) provides broadband wireless communication links that are more flexible than could be provided by a satellite, not to mention cheaper and faster to launch. This is made possible by Raytheon, which, in partnership with Angel Technologies Corporation, has developed ground and airborne electronics necessary for the high-altitude long operation (HALO) network.

The full network includes airborne electronics, as well as ground-based gateways to provide high-speed access to fixed users. The multiple beams on the ground are arranged in a typical cellular pattern, and through frequency re-use, an estimated 2,800 square miles can be covered. The HALO network can provide high-speed data services, including two-way multimedia and Internet connections, without the time and expense normally associated with large installations. In addition, multiple HALO networks can be interconnected, and they can interface with satellites. HALO would have military applications in any rapid-deployment situation where the

Slow Speed Configuration

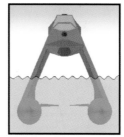
High Speed Configuration

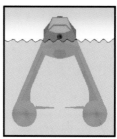
Loiter / Recon Configuration

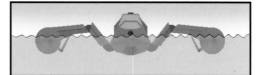
Very Shallow Water Configuration

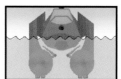
Launch & Recovery Configuration

existing communications network was damaged, destroyed, or under enemy control.

SensorNet Project

The Y-12 National Security Complex at the Oak Ridge National Laboratory (ORNL) is best known for manufacturing and reworking nuclear weapon components, dismantling nuclear weapon components returned from the national arsenal, and serving as the United States' secure storehouse of special nuclear materials—but that's only part of the story.

Other Y-12 programs include the Sensor-Net Project, which is a data architecture and

These illustrations show the various operational configurations in which the CHARC attack craft can operate. *Lockheed Martin*

This artist's conception shows a high-altitude long-operation network (HALO) in service. *Raytheon*

The baseline-like shape and size of the ORNL Banshee siren system make it easily used by United States personnel with little or no training. It was created by an experienced design team with an excellent track record at the Y-12 National Security Complex who are dedicated to support Homeland Security initiatives. *Courtesy Michael Monnett, ORNL*

infrastructure program that supports plug-and-play sensors of various types, as well as archival storage of sensor data and sensor-control services. SensorNet allows for the integration of many dissimilar sensor systems into one "system of systems" infrastructure. SensorNet also provides high reliability of data through the use of self-organizing and self-healing network connectivity, distributed processing, distributed data storage, and backup power supplies.

A wide range of revolutionary SensorNet hardware is being created by an experienced design team Y-12 complex in support of various Homeland Security initiatives. The sensors currently being developed at Y-12 include those detailed in the following four entries.

Banshee

For those not expecting it, the ORNL Banshee truly lives up to its name. This little non-lethal but fearsome weapon is a proposed crowd-dispersal system that consists of a two-inch sensor with a 130-decibel siren encased in rugged, watertight silicon rubber that can be activated and thrown to confuse an approaching enemy or signal a friendly force.

When the trigger is activated, it starts a timing mechanism, allowing an operator time to toss the Banshee. The piercing siren will bounce around, generating a great deal of confusion.

The Banshee is a valuable tool for urban area combat, generating fear and bewilderment in open environments or closed underground facilities. Banshee's application for use in crowd control as a non-lethal weapon is well suited for use by military personnel or first responders, and with slight modification, it can be used in a search and rescue role. Banshee is definitely one of the systems that was developed as part of the

The infrared tactical sensor is a rugged and inexpensive infrared sensor about the size of a button. Like a button, the watertight unit can be sewn onto clothing or attached to equipment to sense above-natural levels of infrared light, invisible to the naked eye, shining toward it. Extreme miniaturization is possible. *Courtesy Michael Monnett, ORNL*

ORNL SensorNet project. The sensor is part of the trigger and timing mechanism; Banshee is not just a bouncing siren.

Infrared Tactical Sensor

ORNL's infrared tactical sensor (ITS) is an inexpensive and extremely lightweight infrared sensor that is designed to be used by an individual person to detect above-natural levels of infrared light, such as is used for targeting missiles or even sniper rifles. A built-in wireless transmitter or a wired connection would alert the individual being scanned. A person wearing it would then hear an audible pulse through an earpiece at variable intervals. As the infrared level intensifies, or as it shines more directly toward the sensor, the pulse frequency would increase to a constant beep, signaling full power, or direct aim.

In addition to being worn by an individual, the ITS could be remotely attached to vehicles, mobile equipment, or motorcades. First responders, VIP security, or other users would be aware of any infrared or visible-light targeting activities. The design concept was developed for military use, but it could be adapted to a wide spectrum of applications to identify imminent threats.

Propelled Tactical Imaging System

Possibly the world's tiniest combat rotorcraft, the propelled tactical imaging system (PTIS) is a small, wireless, wide-angle color-video imaging system propelled for short-distance travel by means of an integral propeller. The propulsion system can be activated manually or by compressed gas to propel the PTIS over walls or to the roofs of nearby buildings. This propulsion system requires no fuel, and it generates neither heat nor excessive noise.

The PTIS imaging system consists of three camera-transmitter systems placed 120 degrees apart, each with a minimum angle of view of 120 degrees. Transmission of its video imagery to an outside source could be sequenced to conserve battery power, or it could be operated live to achieve a real-time 360-degree view from the PTIS landing site. Because its key features are its light weight, small size, and quiet performance, the PTIS is described by ORNL's Y-12 National Security Complex as "appropriate for short-term surveillance of difficult-to-reach or remote areas."

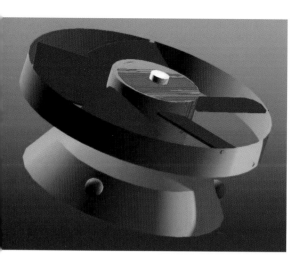

The propelled tactical imaging system is a tiny video imaging system propelled by a tinier integral propeller. It is able to fly quietly and land gently, making it a valuable tool for urban combat and surveillance. *Courtesy Michael Monnett, ORNL*

Solar Tactical Imaging System

Compact and rugged, the solar tactical imaging system (STIS) is a lightweight, wireless video imaging system that can transmit high-resolution color images for miles. It can fit in a pocket and be operational in a matter of seconds. Developed under the ORNL Y-12 SensorNet Program, STIS can be used in any outdoor area requiring video monitoring with minimal preparation and maintenance. As such, it is ideal for any long-term video surveillance in remote areas.

The concept was initially developed for use by foot soldiers as a means of perimeter protection or "eyes backward," allowing them to know of any ongoing activity in their rear area, or to sense whether they were being followed.

STIS is battery powered, but these batteries are charged by a retractable solar panel contained within the body of the system. This ability allows the weatherproof STIS units to perform continuously twenty-four hours per day with no need for external support. Indeed, they can operate unsupervised for weeks or months.

SBIRS High and Low

Dating back to 1996, the space-based infrared system (SBIRS) project evolved out of the SDI-era Brilliant Eyes program discussed earlier. SBIRS involves the development of a galaxy of ballistic-missile-detection spacecraft. The system was envisioned as consisting of SBIRS-High, large satellites deployed 22,000 miles above the earth, and SBIRS-Low, a larger number of smaller satellites in low-earth orbit roughly 621 to 930 miles above the earth. SBIRS-High would detect and track enemy missiles from launch and provide data to defense and interception systems.

The SBIRS-High system consists of spacecraft in geosynchronous earth orbit (GEO) and infrared sensors in highly elliptical orbit (HEO). The HEO payload will scan a large region for ballistic missile launches, and SBIRS operational ground stations will process payload data and report launch events in near real time. Lockheed Martin Space Systems of Sunnyvale, California, is the prime contractor, managing a team that includes Northrop Grumman.

Exoatmospheric Kill Vehicles

Embraced by the Strategic Defense Initiative Office in the 1980s and still an integral weapon in the arsenal of the missile defense agency (MDA), kinetic kill vehicles (KKV) rely on an age-old weapons principle—hit to kill. Like the cave man's club, David's biblical slingshot, or a rifle bullet, KKVs use kinetic energy. They destroy targets through the use of non-explosive projectiles moving at very high speeds. The principal difference between the kinetic weapons of ancient times and those of today's MDA is that is that they do it at hypersonic speeds tens of thousands of feet above the earth. What they do is kill ballistic warheads before they can kill Americans.

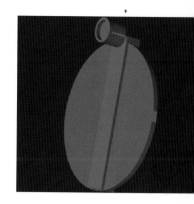

The solar tactical imaging system measures approximately eight by three inches, and weighs about eight ounces. It can be handled and carried by soldiers for surveillance and inspection, or it can be fixed in location using a retractable stand. *Courtesy Michael Monnett, ORNL*

Shown here is the SBIRS GEO pointing and control assembly at the Lockheed Martin facility in Sunnyvale, California, in 2004. The assembly is being prepared for shipment to Northrop Grumman for integration with the payload sensors. *Russ Underwood, Lockheed Martin*

The SBIRS team tests the HEO-1 payload at the Northrop Grumman facility in Azusa, California, prior to shipment to the host for spacecraft integration. The first payload was delivered for integration by Lockheed Martin in August 2004. *Russ Underwood, Lockheed Martin*

In the parlance of national missile defense, KKVs are of two kinds: endoatmospheric kill vehicles, which kill their targets within the atmosphere, and exoatmospheric kill vehicles, which do it above the atmosphere. Early forms of the former included the high endoatmospheric defense interceptor (HEDI) missile, and of the latter, there was the exoatmospheric reentry vehicle interceptor system (ERIS), and the homing overlay experiment (HOE). The HEDI missile was to have been the operational weapons system that evolved from the kinetic kill vehicle integrated technology experiments (KITE) program of the 1980s. It would have been rail-launched in the manner of the Sprint anti-ballistic missiles that dated back to the 1960s.

The current Raytheon exoatmospheric kill vehicle (EKV) is the intercept component of the ground-Based interceptor (GBI), which is in turn the weapon element of the ground-based midcourse defense system. The EKV mission is to engage high-speed ballistic missile warheads in the midcourse phase of flight and to destroy them using hit-to-kill kinetic energy. The EKV uses an infrared seeker to detect and discriminate the incoming warhead from other objects. It also has its own propulsion, communications link, discrimination algorithms, guidance and control system, and computers to support target selection and intercept.

On August 18, 2004, after a series of intercept flight tests (IFT), Raytheon delivered the first deployable flight elements to the MDA from its missile defense kinetic kill vehicle production facility in Tucson, Arizona. These were the first of twenty EKVs scheduled for deployment at Fort Greely, Alaska, and at Vandenberg Air Force Base, California.

"Delivery of the initial EKVs marks a significant milestone in meeting the December 2002 presidential directive to deploy an initial missile defense capability for the United States," said Paul Walker, Raytheon vice president for exoatmospheric kill vehicles. "The delivery of these payloads is the result of the commitment and dedication of employees from both Raytheon and the entire EKV team. Raytheon is proud to provide our fellow citizens with the ability to defend our homeland against the threat of ballistic missiles carrying weapons of mass destruction."

Light Exoatmospheric Projectile

A corollary to the exoatmospheric kill vehicle program discussed above is the RIM-161 light

This payload launch vehicle was used to carry a prototype exoatmospheric kill vehicle (EKV) in a 2001 test launch from Meck Island at the Kwajalein Missile Range. *Department of Defense*

A prototype exoatmospheric kill vehicle (EKV) interceptor is readied for launch at Meck Island at the Kwajalein Missile Range in 2001. Such a vehicle is designed to hit an ICBM more than 140 miles above the earth during the midcourse phase of the warhead's flight. *Department of Defense*

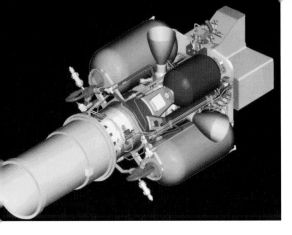

A detailed cutaway illustration of the exoatmospheric kill vehicle (EKV) interceptor. Note that a sizable proportion of the interior volume consists of the fuel and oxidizer tanks. The goblet-shaped retro-rockets provide the EKV with maneuverability in space. *Raytheon*

exoatmospheric projectile (LEAP), also developed by Raytheon. Based on the RIM-156 Standard Block IV SM-2 extended-range missile, the RIM-161 is the missile component of the U.S. Navy theater ballistic missile defense (TBMD) system. Initial LEAP tests conducted in the early 1990s were unsuccessful, but since 2002, the RIM-161 has successfully intercepted ballistic missiles in a new round of evaluations.

The RIM-161 differs from the RIM-156 in that it has three rather than two stages, with the upper stage being powered by an Alliant Techsystems (ATK) Mk.136 solid-fuel rocket. This stage contains a global positioning system and inertial navigation system guidance, as well as a forward-looking infrared (FLIR) sensor to home in on its target.

Kinetic Energy Interceptor

Another current kinetic energy weapon entering the United States Ballistic Missile Defense System arsenal is the aptly-named kinetic energy interceptor (KEI). It is designed to provide a defensive capability against enemy missiles in their boost and ascent phases of flight, when they are the most vulnerable and before their warheads are released. As such, KEI will complement the other interceptor programs that are designed to intercept ballistic missiles in the midcourse and terminal phases of their trajectories. The relative velocity of the KEI intercept would be at hypersonic speeds up to twenty-two thousand miles per hour.

In December 2003, the Missile Defense Agency (MDA) awarded the development and

In this photo, a prototype exoatmospheric kill vehicle (EKV) is launched from Meck Island at the Kwajalein Missile Range on December 3, 2001. At 7:29 P.M. Pacific Standard Time (PST), it would intercept a modified Minuteman intercontinental ballistic missile that had been launched from Vandenberg Air Force Base in California. Impact was at fifteen thousand miles per hour. This flight, designated as IFT-7 (intercept flight test), was the third success of the EKV in five tests. *Department of Defense*

The Raytheon RIM-161 lightweight exoatmospheric projectile (LEAP) is a three-stage ballistic-missile interceptor that is 21.5 feet long, with a diameter of just over a foot. The upper stage is a hit-to-kill kinetic warhead. *Raytheon*

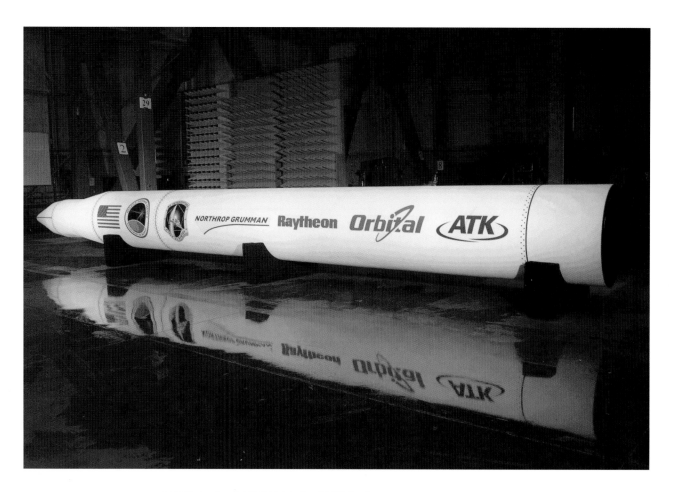

This full-scale mockup of the KEI Interceptor is thirty-six feet long, and thirty-six inches in diameter. Orbital Sciences built the booster, and Raytheon developed the kill vehicle, which will be faster and more agile than any other interceptor. *Orbital Sciences*

Looking every bit like a ballistic missile lurking in its launch silo, this target launch vehicle (TLV) is actually designed merely to mimic a ballistic missile in live-fire tests of anti-ballistic missile systems. It is produced by Orbital Sciences, makers of the booster segment of the KEI Interceptor. *Orbital Sciences*

testing contract for the KEI to a team led by Northrop Grumman. Within the team, Raytheon is responsible for the actual kill vehicle, and Orbital Sciences has responsibility for the booster, with Alliant Techsystems (ATK) building the engine. The divert and attitude control system is by Aerojet. The KEI will operate from a mobile land-based launch vehicle, with command, control, battle management and communications handled from a Humvee. The entire system will be highly mobile and easily transported globally in a single C-17.

Early Light

Located at the Livermore National Laboratory near San Francisco, the National Ignition Facility (NIF) Project is the world's largest laser program. NIF is a key component of the National Nuclear Security Administration's Stockpile Stewardship Program, whose purpose is to maintain the safety, reliability, and effectiveness of the United States' nuclear stockpile without underground nuclear testing. The primary mission of NIF is to attain fusion ignition in the laboratory. This will provide the basis for future decisions about

Inside the world's largest laser project, this view shows the upper portion of the National Ignition Facility target chamber, with beam tubes penetrating through the ceiling. *Lawrence Livermore National Laboratory*

fusion's potential as a long-term energy source. In addition, the high-energy-density regimes accessible though NIF experiments will yield new insight into the origin of our universe.

In July 2001, the National Ignition Facility began working on an accelerated set of projects that led to the NIF Early Light (NEL) ultraviolet laser light program. On May 30, 2003, the NEL program set a world record for laser-beam output performance.

Mobile Tactical High-Energy Laser

When the history of military technology in the early twenty-first century is written, it will certainly be noted that this was the era when one of the most compelling weapons of early-twentieth-century science fiction became fact. The death ray, a ray of light capable of destroying fast-moving projectiles, will become a reality in high-powered lasers.

Even before the Strategic Defense Initiative of the 1980s, the Thompson Ramo Woolridge Company (TRW) and Hughes Aircraft had developed the mid-infrared advanced chemical laser (MIRACL) as an experimental system funded by the United States Department of Defense. First demonstrated in 1980, MIRACL was then the highest-power laser ever built in the Western world. A deuterium fluoride chemical laser, it was also the first megawatt-class continuous-wave laser in the United States.

As with other SDI programs, the MIRACL test program went into hibernation as the Cold War came to a close, only to be quietly revived a few years later. MIRACL reemerged as part of a new program known as tactical high-energy laser/advanced concept technology demonstrator (THEL/ACTD). In June 1996, under this program, MIRACL reportedly became the first laser to successfully shoot down a missile with a death ray.

The mobile tactical high-energy laser (MTHEL) is shown during summer 2004 field tests against incoming artillery at the U.S. Army's High Energy Laser Systems Test Facility (HELSTF) at the White Sands Missile Range in New Mexico. *Northrop Grumman*

The beam director for the demonstrator system of the U.S. Army's tactical high-energy laser (MTHEL), seen here, is the key optical component of the THEL/ACTD pointer tracker subsystem. *Northrop Grumman*

This artist's conception shows how the mobile tactical high-energy laser (MTHEL) might look when deployed to the battlefield. It's a pretty complex setup, but plans are in motion to miniaturize it to be transportable by a single Humvee. *Northrop Grumman*

This test, conducted at White Sands, involved TRW (part of Northrop Grumman after 2002) and the U.S. Army, as well as Israel's Ministry of Defense. The latter was the catalyst for the test, as Israel was looking to develop a defense against the Katyusha surface-to-surface rockets that are frequently fired into Israeli territory from Lebanon and Syria. In October 1997, the new system was used for the first time against an orbiting satellite in a test designed to determine the potential vulnerability of satellites to high-energy lasers.

By 2005, Northrop Grumman was developing a mobile variant of the tactical high-energy laser. The mobile THEL (MTHEL) would be available to battlefield commanders with an effective speed-of-light defense against ballistic and cruise missiles, and air-to-surface munitions. Indeed, the MTHEL was successfully field tested against incoming artillery missiles in May 2004, and against mortar rounds three months later. At the

time of the 2004 tests, high-energy lasers were the only weapon proven effective against artillery. The MTHEL demonstrator was carried in three tractor-trailer trucks, but the plan is to scale the system down so an operational MTHEL could be mounted on a single Humvee.

Solid-State Heat-Capacity Laser

A potential later generation to MIRACL and MTHEL is the solid-state heat capacity laser (SSHCL), an advanced defense system designed and built for the U.S. Army Space and Missile Defense Command by the Lawrence Livermore National Laboratory. It is a prototype of a tactical weapon to be used to protect against incoming artillery shells, antitank missiles, and other projectiles.

The prototype SSHCL that was delivered to the army's White Sands Missile Range in New Mexico in September 2001 used flashlamps powered by an electrical source. These in turn

The solid-state heat-capacity laser is an advanced-defense weapons system being built for the U.S. Army. It is designed to protect against incoming artillery shells, antitank missiles, and other projectiles. *Lawrence Livermore National Laboratory*

pump the nine neodymium-doped glass disks of the amplifier, which then release the energy in pulses of laser light.

The prototype required one megawatt of input power to produce a thirteen-kilowatt laser beam. The average output power was ten kilowatts, and it could deliver five-hundred-joule pulses at twenty hertz in ten-second bursts. These essentially vaporized metal.

SSHCL project manager Brent Dane, of Livermore's Laser Science and Technology program, noted that the ultimate objective of the project is to build a next-generation system with enough electrical efficiency to produce a

one-hundred-kilowatt laser beam from the same one megawatt of input power. The final version will be capable of firing two hundred pulses per second.

An operational SSHCL is being developed by the Livermore team in conjunction with its industrial partners including Raytheon, General Atomics, PEI Electronics, Northrop Grumman, Goodrich Corporation, Armstrong Laser Technology, and SAFT America. Such an operational SSHCL would be used to defend against rockets, artillery, mortars, and other tactical threats at close ranges up to six miles. It could be mounted on, and fired from, a vehicle the size of a common Humvee. The era when a laser capable of melting metal will be routinely deployed is nearer than one might imagine.

Chemical Oxygen-Iodine Laser (COIL)

During the Cold War, lasers were seen by many as the magic bullet of ballistic-missile defense. First conceived under the SDI programs of the 1980s was the idea of a laser weapon that could be fired from an airplane. Like many such programs from the SDI years, this notion was a

The YAL-1A airborne laser aircraft is based on the airframe of a Boeing 747-400F freighter. A major difference in appearance is, of course, the large and prominent nose turret. *Boeing*

The prototype YAL-1A airborne laser aircraft takes off on a flight test from the long runway at Edwards Air Force Base. The flight test program began in 2002. *Boeing*

A Lockheed Martin Space Systems engineer in the company's Sunnyvale, California, facility inspects the turret ball conformal window on the flight turret assembly for the airborne laser. The window is the exit for the high-energy laser, and the exit and return window for the beacon illuminator and tracker illuminator lasers. *Russ Underwood, Lockheed Martin*

Shown here is a surrogate of the first fully integrated flight turret ball for the airborne laser program, being prepared for end-to-end beam-control/fire-control-system integrated testing at Lockheed Martin Space Systems Company in Sunnyvale, California. *Russ Underwood, Lockheed Martin*

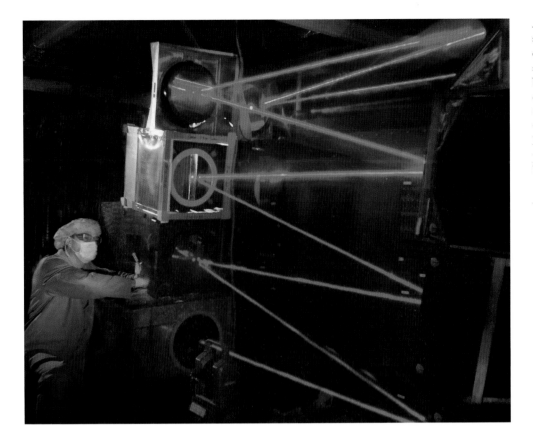

An engineer makes an adjustment to the beam-control optics used to stabilize and shape the beam from the chemical oxygen iodine laser (COIL) on its way to the nose of the airborne laser aircraft, where it is pointed at a target ballistic missile. *Russ Underwood, Lockheed Martin*

staggering technological challenge that would become a reality today. Initiated by the U.S. Air Force in 1996, the high-energy chemical oxygen-iodine laser (COIL) program was the first megawatt-class laser weapons system to be carried on an aircraft. Ultimately, this program would evolve into the airborne laser (ABL), a system designed to autonomously detect, track, and destroy hostile ballistic missiles.

A series of development contracts was issued to the industrial firms that would be known as Team ABL. This team designed an ABL demonstration system that performed a successful boost-phase shoot-down of a theater ballistic missile a decade later. Within this team, TRW (part of Northrop Grumman after 2002) built the COIL itself, while Boeing provided overall program management and systems integration, and modified an aircraft to fly with the laser. Lockheed Martin developed and produced the ABL's target-acquisition, beam-control, and fire-control systems.

The COIL carrier aircraft, designated as YAL-1A, was based on a Boeing 747-400F transport and was built by Boeing in Everett, Washington, near Seattle. It was flown to Boeing's factory in Wichita, Kansas, in January 2000 to be fitted with a controllable nose turret to direct the laser beam. With this installed, flight testing began in July 2002. Meanwhile, Northrop Grumman built and ground tested the COIL in Southern California and delivered it to Edwards Air Force Base in February 2003.

The testing of the airborne laser's beam-control/fire-control (BC/FC) system was completed in April 2004, and Lockheed Martin began final integration of the flight turret assembly, including the 1.5-meter telescope/beam director. The beam-control/fire-control system will accurately point and fire the laser with sufficient energy to destroy the missile while it's still in the highly vulnerable boost phase of flight, before separation of its warheads. The conformal window, the large piece of glass on the forward side of the turret ball, is one of the largest transmissive optics ever coated.

On November 12, 2004, Team ABL fired a laser beam for the first time using the flight laser modules in the ABL System Integration Lab at Edwards Air Force Base. When fully configured, the YAL-1A will serve as the prototype for a family of weapons to defend against the threat of rogue missile attacks in the twenty-first century.

Also by Bill Yenne:

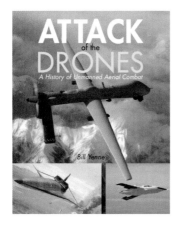

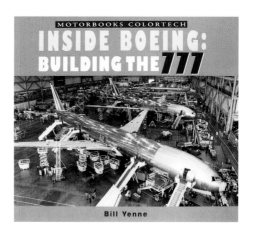

Attack of the Drones
ISBN 0-7603-1825-5

Inside Boeing: Building the 777
ISBN 0-7603-1251-6

Other Zenith Press titles of interest:

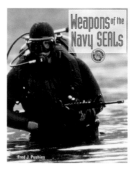

The Spycraft Manual:
The Insider's Guide to Espionage Techniques
ISBN 0-7603-2074-8

Weapons of the Navy SEALs
ISBN 0-7603-1790-9

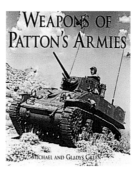

Weapons of the Waffen SS
ISBN 0-7603-1594-9

Weapons of Patton's Armies
ISBN 0-7603-0821-7